How to Grow Fresh Herb Garden Plants:

The Beginner Guide to Growing Herbs in Pots, Planting a Tea Herb Garden and Herb Garden Designs

Author: Kelly D. Minnis

For Cody

ISBN: 1452833702

EAN-13: 9781452833705

Copyright 2010   Kelly D. Minnis

All rights reserved.

The author and publisher of this book have used their best efforts in preparing this book. The author and publisher make no representation or warranties with respect to the accuracy, applicability, fitness, or completeness of the contents of this book. They disclaim any warranties (expressed or implied), merchantability, or fitness for any particular purpose. The author and publisher shall in no event be held liable for any loss or other damages, including but not limited to special, incidental, consequential, or other damages.

This book contains material protected under international and federal copyright laws and treaties. Any unauthorized reprint or use of the material is prohibited.

Table of Contents

Introduction 9
   How to Use This Book Wisely 10
Chapter 1: 13
Why Herbs? 13
   Culinary Herbs 14
   Aromatic Herbs 16
   Ornamental Herbs 16
   Medicinal Herbs 17
   The Ancient Chinese Knew Their Herbs 18
   Prescription Drugs Derived From Herbs 20
   Tea Time 22
Chapter 2 23
Which Herbs? 23
   Top 10 Culinary Herbs 23
   Top 10 Healing Herbs 30
Chapter 3: 43
Design a Garden 43
   Planning Your Garden on Paper 46
   Ideas for Your Garden 47
   Types of Herb Gardens 48
   Formal Gardens 48
   Medieval Gardens 50
   The Botanical Garden 50
   Medieval Gives Rise to Renaissance 50
   Devising Your Culinary Herb Garden 51
   Accents in Your Garden 54
   Grouping Your Plants 55
   Your Private Tea Garden 55
   Accent Your Garden with Tea-Related "Accessories" 56
Chapter 4: 59
Outdoor Gardening 59
   Planting Your Herbs 60
   Alternatives to Hardening Off 62
   Fertilizing Your Herbs 62
   Growing Herbs in Containers 63

- Specific Soil for Certain Herbs 63
- Watering Your Herbs 64
- Diseases, Insects and Other Pests 64
- Companion Plants 65
- More Examples of Companion Plants 65

Chapter 5:
Indoor Gardening 69
- Using Light 70
- Artificial Light 71
- Types of Light 71
- Humidity 73
- Watering 74
- Powdery Mildew 75
- The Actual Planting 76

Chapter 6:
Caring for the Herbs 79
- Surviving a Cold, Hard Winter 80
- Propagating New Plants 81
- Harvesting, Preserving Herbs 82
- Preserving Your Herbs 84
- Time is of the Essence 85
- Drying is Just the Beginning 86
- Storing Your Herbs 86
- Moisture Kills 87
- Freezing Fresh Herbs 87

Conclusion 89

Appendix I 91
What Your Herbs need 91

Appendix II 103
Preparing Herbal Remedies 103
- Tincture Recipe 104
- Herbal Plasters 105
- Poultices 107

References 109
- Web Sites 109
- Books 110

Index 111

> *"Yup, gardening and laughing are two of the best things in life you can do to promote good health and a sense of well being."*
> ***~ David Hobson, The Mad Gardener***

Introduction

Is it the influence of the "Green Movement?" Or is it the growing concern over the economy? Or perhaps it's just the love of herbs have finally gotten hold of enough people to create the interest in herb gardening we see today.

Whatever reason brings you to desire or even consider growing your own herbs – your health, culinary tastes or just plain beauty. Congratulations.

You're about to enter a wonderfully enchanting view of life, where everyday when you wake up and walk on your deck, terrace or backyard, you'll be touched by visual beauty and fragrant vitality.

> *"There can be no other occupation like gardening in which, if you were to creep up behind someone at their work, you would find them smiling". ~Mirabel Osler*

You'll now have the opportunity to create culinary masterpieces, improve your health and that of your family or just enrich your life.

The good news is that herbs are easy to grow. If you provide them with the conditions that they like, most of them actually take the least amount of care in your garden.

And if you're a beginning gardener, then herbs are must-grow items because of that fact alone. Including herbs will give you the confidence you need to go on to more difficult plants.

If on the other hand, you're an experienced gardener, then no doubt you'll appreciate these amazing plants for that very same reason. Once you have established your garden, it takes little effort on your part to get it to look absolutely spectacular and keep it that way (But of course, I encourage you to take all the credit your guests would like to toss your way!)

Of course, it goes without saying that you can just add dabs of colors and textures to an otherwise dreary patch of your flower garden. Many gardeners use herbs to separate flowers whose colors may clash or place them where no flower would succeed in growing.

If you've got a damp, shady spot in your garden where nothing else grows, try an herb. As you delve deeper into this hobby, you'll learn how easy this can be.

Or perhaps you're just interested in planting a few herbs in a couple containers to start. You may want to keep several herbs potted on your back porch. Or maybe you want to grow only a very few of these culinary plants.

How to Use This Book Wisely

This book is designed to help you learn more about the wonderful plants you're about to take on.

Chapter 1 answers the question that's on everyone's mind, "Why herbs?" In this chapter we'll ask you questions about why you're drawn to herb gardening. Your answers reveal not only the type of garden you'll probably end up planting, but the various kinds of herbs you'll probably include within it.

Chapter 2 digs a little deeper (pardon the pun) on the subject of herbs. Once you've taken that step backwards and examined why you want to grow herbs, then you can intelligently decide which herbs you want to grow.

Now granted, your first year of gardening might be a bit of a hit and miss. In a way, if you're truly successful at gardening, it will be. Once you start learning about herbs, you really won't want to stop. By the end of your initial growing season, you'll have a list of half a dozen or more herbs you'll want to include in your next venture.

Part of this chapter is devoted to providing you with some of the most popular herbs, both used in culinary practices as well as for healing purposes. Of course, you'll soon discover that strict classification of these is nearly impossible.

Take basil for example. Typically, people think of basil as a culinary delight, but the bonus in growing this plant is its ability to work wonders as an anti-inflammatory remedy. If you decide to grow basil for its flavor, you may end up using it for your health as well.

And that brings us to Chapter 3. You are taking charge of your herb garden, from the ground up. In Chapter 3, "Design a Garden" is devoted to helping you decide not only what type of garden you'd like to begin with, but how to bring the vision to life. We explore your options and discuss what works best for your lifestyle and personal culinary and health needs.

Should you decide to cultivate an outdoor garden, I've got you covered in Chapter 4. It's here I give you the low-down on how to successfully raise herbs in your own yard. Filled with hints, tips, and suggestions, you'll find this chapter to be a great jumpstart to your hobby.

If you'd rather start with an indoor garden (or as many people do, a combination of both) then you'll want to make sure you read Chapter 5. The information contained in this chapter will ensure that your first indoor herbal expedition will be nothing less than successful.

And that brings us to Chapter 6, which is a general overview of the best methods to keeping your herbs healthy, happy, and strong. If you've got any doubts at all about whether you can maintain herbs, this chapter was written to reassure you that, "Yes you can!"

If you need to know just a little bit about specific herbs, then turn to Appendix I, where I've compiled a list of specific herbs, the best methods to propagate them and what kind of environment they grow best in.

And finally, Appendix II provides you with a little more information on preparing health-giving remedies, using the herbs from your garden. You'll discover what a tincture and a poultice are. Then, more importantly, learn how to make and use them to help alleviate the minor symptoms of some of the most common health problems.

Enjoying an herb garden is one of life's luxuries. But maintaining it shouldn't be a burden. In fact, you'll find once you dig into this book, how wonderfully relaxing, and even therapeutic, this marvelous hobby can be.

So don't waste another minute. Start now deciding on what form your herb garden will take. Happy gardening!

Chapter 1:

Why Herbs?

> *Answering the question <u>why</u> you want to grow herbs inevitably leads to which herbs to grow.*

Before you take the shovel or plant a single herb, stop to consider why you want an herb garden. What are your intentions for planting these marvelous plants?

Are you planning on using them both fresh and dried for culinary purposes to add to your meals and enhance the flavors? Are you planning on making flavored oils or vinegars to present to friends and family members as gifts (while keeping a couple stashed for yourself?)

Or have you discovered the many natural health benefits of herbs and would like to grow your own to brew teas, infusions, or pastes to use to help your minor health conditions?

The reasons to grow herbs are important. First, you may be planting totally different plants if your aim is to embolden your entrees than you would to empower your health.

But beyond just the uses of herbs, you must at some point decide on a size for your garden. As you read through this book, I'll show you some lavish designs for herb gardens that consume entire back yards.

Perhaps you don't want to start quite that big though. So I'll also show you smaller container gardens grown both indoors or out. Then I'll show you an alternative where you can grow just a few herbs, keeping them modestly small and manageable and well within reach, right on your kitchen windowsill.

Whatever you choose, be prepared to make choices and plenty of them. Of course, this may sound overwhelming at first. But you arrive at this place knowing your intentions, perhaps well-armed with the names of a few herbs hoping to include some of your favorites.

And hopefully, you'll discover a few more herbs you hadn't initially considered. After all, that's the true joy of herb gardening – watching something unexpected spring up.

Culinary Herbs

For many people, this class of herb is the most recognizable and the most useful. Even those who have never used an herbal supplement in their life know what some fresh basil can do to a meal, or the difference some oregano can make in spaghetti sauce, or how some fresh chives can make a baked potato come to life.

But, then when asked to define a *culinary herb,* many of us are quite lost. "Why of course, you know what an herb is," you say, trying to back out of reciting a strict definition. Let me help you out.

Culinary herbs – sometimes referred to as sweet herbs – are those plants (whether they are annual, biennial or perennial) that have tender roots or ripe seeds. They also possess an aromatic scent and have a great flavor.

If you think that you're among the first generation to discover some of these herbs, I hate to disappoint you. As long as mankind has been eating, womankind (not to be sexist, though) has been literally spicing up cooking with herbs. Paleontologists have discovered the ancient Egyptians used herbs even before the pharaohs ordered the building of the pyramids.

Similarly, the ancient Chinese naturally turned to the plants in their gardens in order to enhance the flavor and appearance of their meals.

And of course, you need look no further than the Bible to see how herbs were not only used, but actually prized by many. Read through the books of Matthew and Luke. You'll find references to tithes paid in herbs like mint, cumin, and other herbs deemed valuable.

Now take a quick look at the Old Testament. More than 700 years before the birth of Christ, Isaiah talks about sowing and threshing cumin. And since it's used in the same reference and grown in the same fields as barley and wheat, you just take for granted that it's used for culinary purposes.

Unfortunately, the use of these specialty herbs has lost the general appeal that has kept wheat, barley and even rye the staples of cooking. And that's a shame.

> *"My green thumb came only as a result of the mistakes I made while learning to see things from the plant's point of view."*
> *~H. Fred Dale*

Perhaps only one herb has really kept its status among cooks as a must-have and that's parsley. Today few of us are even aware that such herbs as hyssop, rue or horehound exist, let alone use them daily in our cooking.

If mankind in general had kept pace seriously cultivating some of these herbs, then the flavors of them could have been remarkably improved throughout history. And consequently would make cooking today even more exciting.

But mankind's loss is your gain. Since some herbs are so difficult to find, growing them yourself is really your only option. And now, you have the wonderfully thrilling chance of growing these in your own back yard or even right on your windowsill.

Aromatic Herbs

While some of these may include culinary herbs, *aromatic herbs* usually are grown to be used as additives in products such as perfumes, toilet water and other items needing a radiant fragrance.

If you're like many other herb growers, this is not the primary reason for growing herbs. Few herbalists cultivate for this reason. But that's not to say that your finished results won't create a stunning effect in your garden because they absolutely will.

Like their culinary cousins, aromatic herbs have a long, rich history that goes just as far back as the culinary plants. The ancient Egyptians, were perhaps the most well known of peoples to use herbs. And they were especially known for the creation of a fragrance called Kyphi. Today, we would classify it as "incense." This fragrance was widely used in religious services as part of an overall purification ceremony.

Today you may be growing them to use intact, perhaps to scent your linens or items of clothing. Consider drying plants like marjoram, lovage, rosemary and even basil and you'll discover that their precious scents linger for a long time.

Ornamental Herbs

Your desire to grow herbs may simply be to create a dazzling environment. No doubt, you've seen the brightly colored flowers and foliage of many of these gorgeous plants. Some have less color and more pastel or even whitish looking flowers.

These are classified as *ornamental herbs*, whose sole purpose is to be decorative. Of course there may be some overlapping. Some culinary herbs are very beautiful as they grow. Many medicinal herbs are also stunning to behold.

Ornamental herbs may be beautiful not because of their colors, but simply for the texture of the leaves. These plants make perfect accents for a balcony or to line your flower bed.

And if your main purpose is for ornamental or decorative reasons, you may never harvest these plants.

If you're considering adding herbs to your world for this reason you'll find that valerian, which is also a very valuable medicinal herb, is a perfect choice. It carries crimson blossoms. Borage and chicory are also good choices here with their blue flowers. But don't overlook other herbs that could add delightful color including variegated thyme, Mint lavender and even chives.

Another perfect example of an ornamental herb is one called the "Dittany of Crete". It's a type of oregano. Forming a low mound and producing leaves with fine silvery hairs, this plant wasn't made to add flavor to any meal. It was created just to be admired!

Medicinal Herbs

Perhaps of all the classifications of herbs, no history is more interesting than that of *medicinal herbs*. Our ancestors at one time prized these plants. Sometimes they were the only tools that stood between them and death. In eras gone by, when medical knowledge was either nonexistent or in its infancy, every family had at least on amateur herbalist in its family tree.

Herbal medicine is, without a doubt, the oldest form of "healthcare" known to the human species. You can't find one culture throughout history (and you can travel as far back in time as you like) that didn't use some plants to treat the ill members of its society.

Even primitive humans at the very least observed and appreciated the many different kinds of plants that were available to them to help heal their family. It's a shame we don't have some record of how the first man (or perhaps more appropriately, woman) realized that plants possessed that healing power.

However they discovered it, paleontologists have found evidence of their use. Alongside the bones of a Stone Age - era man in Iraq, for example, some thoughtful relative had tucked a few herbs. Most notably the herbs *marshmallow root,* hyacinth and *yarrow* were buried with him.

Today marshmallow root is used to soothe inflammations like a sore throat. Hyacinth is used as a diuretic which encourages tissues to release any excess water they may be retaining. And yarrow is a cold and fever remedy that was just about everywhere in its use prior to the creation of aspirin.

The Ancient Chinese Knew Their Herbs

A testimony to our great debt to our ancestors' amazing knowledge of herbs stands on a treatise, written by the Chinese emperor Shen Nong, circa 2735 BC.

In this treatise, which is still used to this very day, he recommended a herb called *ma huang.* You may be more familiar with it in its Western name – Ephedra. This herb, he explained more than 2300 years before the birth of Christ, is an excellent remedy to alleviate the signs of respiratory distress.

Today, we have a medication called *Ephedrine*, extracted from this herb, that's widely used as a decongestant. In its synthetic form it's called *Pseudoephedrine* and you can find it in many allergy sinus and cold medications today. Imagine that nearly 5,000 years ago this plant was recognized as a potential healer.

It's very possible, from the little that historians know and can piece together, that our ancestors deciphered the plants' healing powers by simply watching the actions of the animals around them.

While for the most part the passing on of this information is strictly verbal in nature, you'll find several herbalists who recorded some information. This is especially true in monasteries. Surprisingly, many monks, priests and nuns were very adept at medicinal herbalism.

More likely than not, the specific knowledge of these herbs were passed down from one generation to another. You can almost hear a grandmother instructing her granddaughter now, as they stand in the herb garden:

> *"You want to be sure to pick this plant when it's at its greenest. And you'll want to use this one here when you get a headache. And then, you'll only want the leaves and stems."*

If you're a budding herbalist then you probably already know that depending on the plant, the health problem and the remedy, you'll use various parts of your homegrown plants. You may use the leaves, flowers, stems, or fruits from certain plants and their roots to relieve symptoms or to even prevent certain health conditions from ever occurring.

Prescription Drugs Derived From Herbs

While some in the medical community may look down on the use of herbs as foolish at best (and dangerous at its worst), remember that many of today's most effective prescription drugs began as herbs. The active ingredients in these herbs were then isolated and duplicated synthetically. Some of today's most effective heart medications owe their success to their direct "herbal ancestor."

Even the revered (and versatile) A*spirin* began as the bark of the white willow tree. Scientists then isolated what exactly made the willow so remarkably effective, reproduced the ingredient synthetically and the world's most popular over-the-counter drug was developed.

Before the discovery and widespread use of antibiotics, the herb e*chinacea* (which many know better as the *Purple Coneflower*) was one of the most widely prescribed medicines in the United States.

Today, it's making a comeback for its outstanding ability to help boost the immune system. Many individuals take this herb in a capsule or tablet form in order to fend off colds and flu throughout the long, winter months.

Today's modern research has confirmed this plant's ability to strengthen your immune system. Active ingredients in this herb actually stimulate the production of much-needed "disease-fighting" white blood cells.

> *"The garden is the poor man's apothecary."* ~German Proverb

So what's the bottom line to all of this? If you plan on growing herbs for their medicinal or healing qualities, you'll not only want to know which herbs can help alleviate specific symptoms, but you'll want to learn exactly how to use these herbs.

We've already mentioned the herb echinacea as a healing herb. This is in fact one of the easiest of all medicinal herbs to grow -- and perhaps one of the prettiest. This flower, native to the central and eastern United States, resembles a daisy in structure. They have an extended period of bloom, making them a nice resident in your garden.

The echinacea plant begins to bloom in the spring, and continues to spread joy throughout the summer, even lasting into to fall months. It's a hardy plant which can survive droughts as well as handle the very hot summer.

Echinacea looks gorgeous just about anywhere you want to plant them, whether it's in the middle of a garden, along its border, in a rock garden or even in containers.

If you choose echinacea, just keep in mind that it's a tall plant which grows to a height of a little more than two to four feet. But, if you'd prefer a shorter version, then the *Pixie Meadowbrite Coneflower* grows only to a height of a foot and half or so. A true dwarf, you'll love its profusion of pink flowers. You may want to mix that strain with another dwarf, *Kim Knee High Coneflower*, which has purplish-pink flowers and dense foliage.

If you're interested in growing herbs you may already have an idea of the best ways to prepare them in order to receive the maximum amount of natural healing.

If you're not quite that far in your research, then read about some of the really nifty ways you can use herbs to help improve your health, sometimes without resorting to harsh chemically based prescription drugs.

Once you're growing your own herbs, then you have that delightful freedom of using them in a variety of ways. I've included an Appendix in the back of the book on how to effectively use your newly grown medicinal herbs. In that you'll find step-by-step procedures for preparing your plants in a variety of ways.

Tea Time

If you enjoy a nice, quality cup of tea, then you've no doubt dreamed of growing your own plants to steep and enjoy in the mid-afternoon, or a relaxing cup before bedtime.

If you decide to plant herbs to enjoy a "tea garden" you can rest assured that you are continuing a treasured, historic pastime. The tradition dates back not just centuries, but literally thousands of years.

The Chinese and Japanese cultures have been doing this for as long as anyone can remember. Not only did they drink tea, but these cultures created niches to enjoy this beverage undisturbed.

But that doesn't mean the Europeans didn't have their share of tea gardens. The most well-known of the tea drinkers, the English, have created formal and cottage gardens exclusively for the growing of various teas.

But if you love tea, then without a doubt, you've wanted to experience what it would be like if, for once, your tea leaves didn't come packaged in a box and surrounded by a bag.

Now that you have a better idea of why you'd like to start an herb garden, you can then continue your thoughts with what herbs you'd like to grow. It seems like only a logical transition. And it's the topic of the next chapter.

Chapter 2

Which Herbs?

> *Now that you've established the purpose of your herb garden you can make some choices about exactly which herbs you'll include.*

I'll bet you're definitely getting excited now. You can't wait to start your own garden. You can smell the aromatic plants growing in your back yard or your kitchen windowsill. You can even visualize yourself reaching for some fresh herbs to add to your ingredients as you prepare your dinner.

But, as you drive to the nursery to choose your plants, you're still puzzled about which ones exactly to grow. I can understand your confusion. When I first began planting herbs, I experienced the same uncertainty.

That's why I've developed what I call my "Top 10 List of Must-Grow Herbs." These are not only some of the most commonly used herbs in cooking but they also represent some of the easiest ones to grow. And in this list I've also provided the types of soil and other essential growing conditions for success.

Top 10 Culinary Herbs

With this list in hand on your first trip to the nursery, you're bound to have success in finding what will not only work in your yard, but choices that will mesh well with your taste buds.

1. Basil

Basil is the best herb for pesto, hands down. Its leaves have a warm and spicy flavor. You need to only add a small amount of this delightful herb in dishes such as soups, salads and sauces. Basil is also particular suited to season any dish with tomato flavoring. Don't hesitate to use basil to enhance the flavor of your meat, poultry or fish. You can even add it to your morning breakfast omelet.

You'll want to start your basil plants early in the spring, preferably in a greenhouse or a sun-filled windowsill. Early in the summer, transplant this herb to your garden. Or, if you have the courage, sow basil seeds directly into your garden early in the spring. You may want to try your hand at both methods, just in case those seeds don't sprout.

2. Chives

Who doesn't love some fresh *chives* on a hot, freshly-baked potato? If you're as crazy about this herb as me, then you've already noticed that chives have a mild onion taste. This makes them an excellent addition to salads, any egg and cheese dishes, cream cheese, sandwich spreads and sauces. And, by the way, don't restrict chives to just the baked potato. Taste how it adds a little zing to your mashed potatoes as well.

If you plan on growing chives from starter plants, then you'll want to get these into your garden in the early spring. And you'll want to give these plants plenty of room. My recommendation is to plant them a good 9 to 12 inches from each other.

If you plan to plant chive seeds, then plant them in the fall or the spring, digging down a good half inch and setting the seeds in rows that are spaced about 12 inches apart.

3. Coriander

Now here's a versatile herb. Its versatility is so great that different parts of this plant are known as different herbs. Grinding the dried seeds to use them in your meats, like veal, ham or pork? You're using *coriander*. Using the leaves to add to some Indian or Asian dishes? You're actually using *cilantro*.

And of course, you can use the roots of coriander as well. If you can't use them right away, don't worry, you can freeze them. They can be used to flavor soups or chop the roots and serve with avocados. You'll find this delicious.

Even a novice herbalist should have no problem growing coriander from seeds.

Sow these seeds in the early spring. Dig a hole about ¼ inch in depth. Plant them in rows that are just about a foot apart. Once the seedlings appear, you'll want to thin them down some, making sure they are at least 6 inches from each other.

4. Dill

Here's another herb where you can use both the seeds and the leaves. Both of these parts have a sharp, slightly bitter taste.

Whether you use it fresh or dried, you'll find *dill* a most tasty addition to fish, meat and poultry dishes. But don't be afraid to add it to salads and soups as well. Many people use the leaves in potatoes and even in omelets.

Another way to enjoy the unique taste of this herb is to sprinkle a little dill on sliced cucumbers for use as a sandwich filling.

Dill is another easy plant to grow from seed. Plant your seeds in the early spring, about ¼ inch deep. You'll want to make sure you leave at least 9 inches between these seeds. Once the seedlings appear, be sure to thin them, keeping them 9 inches apart.

5. *Fennel*

Like fish? Then you'll have to try *fennel* the next time you create that delectable sauce for your fish. You can also use it for with pork and veal. Many individuals love to use fennel in soups and salads as well.

The leaves themselves have a sweet flavor. The seeds, though, have a sharper flavor to them.

Want to try your hand at growing fennel from seeds? It's easy enough to do. Plant your seeds in groups of three or four around mid-spring. Dig a small hole about a ¼ inch deep. Place the seeds about a foot and a half apart. Once these grow into seedlings, you'll want to thin them.

6. *Mint*

Ah, what would an herb garden be without *mint*? Mint is an essential herb whether you plant a culinary or medicinal Herb garden (or a little of both!).

Use the leaves to brew into a nice, satisfying hot tea. Or use them to add a dash of sunshine to cold drinks as well. Mint also makes a great garnish. Spearmint, specifically, is used to make a mint sauce or jelly.

Mint has historically been the spice of choice for anyone who's preparing lamb. Sprinkle the dried or fresh leaves over the meat prior to cooking it.

You'll want to start planting your mint in the autumn or spring. You'll also have the best results if you begin with the actual roots of the plants. Plant four to six-inch pieces of the root. Make sure they're about two inches deep and a good 12 inches apart.

Then make water them well. Check the roots occasionally. They are quite aggressive. By this, I mean they seem to easily overtake the roots of neighboring plants. You can easily prevent this by sinking boards or bricks about one-foot deep around the beds.

You may also take an extra precaution when you first plant them. Plant them in the garden bed itself, but enclose a plastic bucket (with no bottom) around it. That keeps them contained for a specific depth.

7. Parsley

Parsley makes a great addition to salads, casseroles and omelets. And of course, it's an attractive garnish for meat and fish, as well as any dish that features onions.

If you're planning on growing the plant from seed, start planting them in mid-spring if you want to use the herb in the summer. Plant the seeds in mid-summer if you want fresh autumn and winter parsley.

Before you plant the seeds, you'll need to soak them overnight. When this plant reaches seedling stage thin the bed out and make sure the plants are between nine to 10 inches apart.

8. Sage

If you've ever eaten sweet sausage with *sage,* then you know how awesome this herb can be in culinary enhancement. The dried leaves of the sage plant are also a traditional addition to chicken and turkey stuffing. Many chefs additionally use sage with lamb and pork as well as a variety of cheese and omelet dishes.

Sage is another plant that can easily be grown from its seeds. You'll want to start planting in the early spring if you plan on doing this.

If you prefer, though, you can use starter plants from your local nursery. If you're going this route, you can wait until mid-spring to set them out. Just be sure to plant them about one-foot apart.

9. Tarragon

If you think anything like I do, you hear the word *tarragon* and immediately think vinegar. And it is a great flavoring for vinegar.

Up until now you may have run to the store to buy your tarragon vinegar. But consider waking up one morning, picking some tarragon from your garden, placing it in vinegar, steeping it for two to three weeks and then enjoying your own homemade tarragon vinegar!

But vinegar is just the start of how this plant can dramatically change your eating habits, given a little time and experimentation. The leaves of this herb have a taste that is something akin to *anise,* which makes it ideal for a variety of dishes. Try placing the leaves in soups and stews. From there you can experiment with salads.

But don't let your use of this versatile herb stop there. Think egg dishes as well as any type of soft cheese dish. Let your imagination soar when it comes to your use of tarragon.

This is another herb that seems to have been made especially to season lamb. If lamb isn't your meat of choice, you can still enjoy the flavorful benefits of tarragon with fish, steak and even vegetables.

However, when you grow this herb, steer clear of trying to do it from seeds. You just won't have any luck. Instead, visit your local nursery and buy some small plants.

You'll dig and plant these in early spring, making sure they have lots of room to grow. In this case, give them at least 18 inches from one another.

10. Thyme

Yes, *thyme*. And no, I have no idea why we have to spell it this way. But despite its awkward spelling, and its fame as a starring role in an old Simon and Garfunkel song, growing thyme is a *must* for any self-respecting herbalist.

Thyme is a great seasoning for just about any meat. Rub the chopped fresh leaves (you can also use dried leaves) onto lamb, pork, veal or even beef before you put it in the oven.

This herb also goes to work for you in various other capacities too. Consider adding it to egg or cheese dishes as well as vegetables. And don't be afraid to experiment with it on your fish or poultry either. You'll be pleasantly surprised.

Once you've tried all that, use thyme as a great seasoning for soups, stews, stuffing and even rice.

I even know one person who brews her thyme to make tea. She just adds a bit of rosemary and a sprig of mint to go with it.

You can start this herb from seeds. Sometime in mid-spring make shallow rows for the seeds about one foot apart. When the thyme seedlings are established, then you'll thin them out, placing them about six inches apart.

If you don't feel up to starting thyme from seeds, you'll want to plant your nursery-bought seedlings about mid-spring, again keeping them at least six inches apart (preferably nine inches if you have the room.)

Don't Be Afraid to Actually *Use* Your Herbs . . .

Using your herbs regularly in cooking has two distinct advantages. First, of course, it adds an added dimension to your cooking that not only will impress you, but your spouse and even your children.

But using these herbs regularly, you'll also effectively be keeping your plants shaped nice and growing healthy.

If you're not quite sure what herbs go with which foods, wing it! That's right, just experiment. Oh, you could look it up on the web to get all the "authoritative" answers. But by experimenting with different herbs in various dishes, you may hit upon a combination that's perfect for you.

A word of advice here though: start small and then increase gradually. Fresh herbs are much stronger than the bottled version you buy in the store. So, a little goes a long way.

Besides, it's much easier to add more of a specific herb to a dish.

But if you're ever in doubt about how much to use -- just use your sense of sight. When the herb is flecked evenly throughout your chosen dish, you probably have enough!

Top 10 Healing Herbs

So you want to try your hand at a few of those herbs you've read about and used in various forms to help improve your health. But, you haven't fully decided about all the plants to be included in your garden.

While you're making that decision, let me supply you with some of the most popular of the herbs. Not only have I included the herb, and the growing conditions that it likes the best, I've also included how it may improve your health.

Here's my "Top 10 List" of medicinal herbs for gardeners. Some of these are fairly common, some of them you may not have heard about unless you know your healing herbs and a few may come as a surprise to you!

1. Nettles

Easy to grow, the *nettles* plant family has been used for generations (and then some) as an effective aid against inflammation due to allergies, Arthritis and even Lupus. It's also been used successful as a tonic for helping alleviate the symptoms of Anemia.

And no wonder it's effective. It's rich in iron and vitamin C. Herbalists not only use the leaves of this plant, but they also put the roots to good use treating symptoms as well.

But that's not all, because the plant is abundant in various antioxidants, as well as flavonoids, all health-giving properties that medicine is only now beginning to appreciate.

When harvesting this plant for medicinal purposes, you'll want to be sure that the ones you choose are "sticky." This indicates the presence of resin which is its active healing ingredient.

Sometimes called s*tinging nettles*, you'll want to be sure to wear gloves when you harvest this plant. It packs a good sting which, while harmless, still hurts. And you'll find that you can harvest nettles several times throughout the year.

Nettles are also a plant that "reseeds" itself, which is wonderful because you'll have access to it all year round. Be careful where you plant this herb though. If not pruned back, this plant grows to over six feet, which means it may just squeeze out some other plants in your garden.

If you begin your first season by growing nettles from seeds, be sure to germinate them for 10 to 14 days even before you place them in the ground. Keep the seeds at room temperature. Start your planting in the spring.

Then transplant the seedlings to an area where they receive full sun and just partial shade. Keep the plants at least eight inches from each other, and preferably 12 inches.

2. *Calendula*

This plant, with its bright flowers, is an important part of any healer's garden. Never heard of it? Ah, but I'm betting you've seen it. You probably called it a *marigold*. That's right! It's also called the c*alendula* and is one of the most versatile healing herbs available.

Starting with its striking orange bloom, which is used by many as a soothing skin wash, a tea and a salve, this plant is a staple in my herb garden.

The flower is also edible, so feel free to brighten up your next salad by garnishing it with calendula. The overall gentle healing qualities of this plant makes it a great ingredient for, you guessed it, diaper salves as well as other baby-related skincare items.

Scientific studies show that the calendula may actually help stimulate your immune system and support improved microcirculation, that is the circulation of your blood right down to those tiny capillaries!

The calendula is easy to grow from seeds. Plant the seeds early in the spring and cover them lightly with about a quarter-inch of garden soil. Once the seedlings pop up, you'll want to transplant them so they are about 15 inches from each other.

You'll discover that they germinate early as well as grow quite quickly. And you'll be pleasantly surprised they produce their very first blooms by mid-summer.

The best part of this wonderful plant is that it reseeds itself. Once you've planted them the first time, they will grow for years as long as you don't disturb them.

Calendula loves rich, well-drained soil, but they're hardy and they can live in just about any type of soil. While they may sound like the perfect herb (a gorgeous flower, many healing qualities and a hardiness to survive just about any terrain) the plant does have one drawback. They attract insects.

Aphids seem especially found of this plant. But don't let that discourage you. Simply wash the plant with an insecticidal soap or spray it with a repellant. Before you bring them indoors, make sure you inspect thoroughly for the presence of these insects.

3. *Burdock*

You may be hard pressed to find this herb in most gardens, but including it in yours will make your garden all the more distinctive. Sometimes this herb is referred to as *gobo*, but if you haven't heard it used as either name, I'm not really surprised.

Burdock tea, moreover, is beneficial for your gastrointestinal tract as well as is used by many to boost a slacking appetite. Herbalists have also used this tea to help restore liver function.

Though not native to this country, burdock grows freely in many areas. It was brought over by the original settlers during early colonial times.
Most people start burdock from seed. Start planting in the early spring, the earlier the better, in fact. Cover the seeds with one half to one quarter inch of fine garden soil or seed-starting soil. If the water seems dry when you plant, then you'll want to water it as well.

The seeds germinate quickly, so you should notice some sprouts in about four to seven days. Take the seedlings and thin them until they're about three inches apart, in rows separated by at least two feet. This plant prefers the full sun, but is hardy enough to tolerate some shade as well.

If you're considering growing burdock then you also need to consider the soil in which you place it. This plant needs a rich well-drained soil. The soil itself should be loose and definitely free from rocks and stones.

And that's not just on the surface. Be sure that the area below this plant is rock-free for at least several feet in depth. This allows the burdock's root to take hold securely as it does have a big, strong root.

And yes, you can eat this herb too. Pick the leaves when they are quite tender, and then cook them just like you would spinach.

If you're planning on using the roots as a medicinal tool, you'll have to wait for a while. They take a good long time to grow. Some herbalists say you need to wait about 100 days.

Don't pick the roots before they are two feet long. Then simply peel them. You may either eat the root raw or cook it.

Many people use the root in soups, salads and even in stir-fry dinners.

4. Chamomile

This is perhaps one of the best known of all the healing herbs, thanks to the commercialization, marketing and popularity of *chamomile* tea. You may already buy and drink this tea prior to going to sleep at night, or when your nerves seem agitated. The plant is best known for its calming effects on the human body.

And more recently, scientific studies from England are conferring additional healing powers on this already beloved plant. Drinking chamomile tea may do more than just make you sleepy. It could also boost your immune system, making you more resistant to colds and the flu as well as other infections.

But did you realize that you can grow this fascinating herb and make your own tea? And use the plant in several other ways to help your system as well?

This herb is easy to grow from seed. It loves the full sun and does well in average soil, but really thrives in a rich environment. You'll want to plant your seeds in the spring. Once they grow into seedlings, thin them to 15 to 18 inches from each other.

They require little care. When harvesting this herb, you'll want to wait until the flowers reach their peak bloom. For remedies, you can use the plant either fresh or dried. Drying of the flowers is quite easy. Simply spread them out in a cool and well-ventilated place. That's all you need to do!

Use the flowers to brew the tea. You can also add the flowers to other kinds of tea to make a light and refreshing blend. You can serve this hot or cold, or be imaginative and serve in a punch.

> ## The Secret Life of . . .
>
> When is an herb not an herb? When it's a weed!
>
> I couldn't bring myself to include this in the suggestions to plant in your herb garden, but at the same time, I couldn't pass up telling you about the amazing secret life of the dandelion.
>
> Didn't know that the dandelion is also a prized herb? This lowly plant, disdained by nearly all of us, is probably one of the most versatile healing herbs you can find.
>
> Take the familiar flower of the dandelion to help ease those throbbing, aching muscles. The leaf and root are used in various forms to help with both skin and muscle problems.
>
> But that's not all, because you can also use the flower and leaves in salads. The flower, additionally, makes a great jelly.
>
> And who hasn't heard of dandelion wine?

5. *Echinacea*

Definitely give this healing herb a chance in your healing garden. You've no doubt heard about the wonderful properties of this plant. *Echinacea* has been noted for the last several years as a powerful booster for your immune system.

Many individuals take this herb in capsule or tablet form as a supplement, especially during the winter months, to avoid contracting colds and the flu during the winter months.
This plant, with its large, bright flower is also known as the purple coneflower. There are three distinct varieties of echinacea: *echinacea pallid, echinacea angustifolia* and *echinacea pupuea.* All three have similar medicinal effects.

This plant is also used for respiratory infections by many herbalists. In Europe, it's not unusual for medicinal doctors to prescribe this to their patients for a variety of remedies.

You might think with all these wonderfully effective health benefits, echinacea would be near impossible to grow (aren't we conditioned to believe there's a catch behind every good thing?). Well nothing could be further from the truth. It's actually quite easy to grow. One of the most amazing aspects of their success is their tolerance for dry conditions.

And you can actually grow this amazing plant from seed with little trouble. Plant the seeds when your soil reaches between 55 to 70 degrees Fahrenheit in the spring.

You need do nothing more initially than sow the seeds on the surface. Within 10 to 20 days, you should notice the seeds germinating. Once this happens, then you'll cover them with about one-eighth of an inch of soil.

When they reach the seedling stage, you'll want to thin the plants so they're about 18 to 24 inches apart.

This plant prefers shade over full sun. You may also want to test your soil's pH balance before planting your seeds. This plant prefers neutral soil, with a rating of six to eight.

Echinacea blooms from June to October. And they attract the most beautiful of butterflies! Even if you don't use the plant for health reasons, its presence in your garden lifts your spirit when you watch the butterflies hover around it!

6. Lavender

No herbal healing garden would be complete without at least a small place dedicated to *lavender*. Lavender is to healing pain what echinacea is to the immune system: indispensible!

One of the most effective topical creams I've ever used had lavender as its main herbal ingredient.

The health benefits of lavender are many. In addition to relieving pain, it's noted for it relaxing effects, the remarkable ability to relieve anxiety. Partly because of this ability, it's used by many as a "cure" for Insomnia as well as a muscle relaxant.

But beyond that, there may be some hard scientific evidence that lavender may also help support healthy blood pressure levels.

If you're not familiar with what the plant looks like, you'll recognize it once you see it. It has needle-like foliage that's bluish-grey in color, topped with violet-blue slender-looking flowers. The long-blooming flowers are sure to delight you throughout the entire growing season.

This plant is, thankfully, drought tolerant, making it easy to care for. Don't try to start this herb from seed though. Your best bet is to go to your nursery to buy a flat of small plants that were cuttings from another plant.

If you insist on trying your hand at starting lavender from seed, then grow the seeds in small pots early in the spring. The drawback with this method is that the seeds may die before they fully germinate.

Even if you get some seeds to survive, the next obstacle you need to overcome is the slow sprouting of the seeds which, in some cases, takes more than two weeks. This invites the growth of fungus on the small plants. In some cases, these poor things actually rot before they get the chance to grow.

Once you have a successful plant in your garden, make sure it's in an area that is well drained.

7. Lemon Balm

Here's another staple of every healing herb garden. Originally native to southern Europe, *lemon balm* is now found everywhere on the globe.

Its medicinal traits are similar to those of mint. It produces a positive effect on the digestive system, for starters. This herb is also used to relive pain and discomfort that usually comes with indigestion. Individuals who suffer from anxiety, nervousness as well as mild insomnia also use this plant with much success.

The most common method of using the medicinal healing powers of this plant is through steeping the leaves for tea.

Part of the mint family, lemon balm grows to be about a foot to a foot and a half tall, and has a small two-lipped flower that blooms in the late summer. And as you might guess from its name, its leaves have a definite aroma and flavor of lemon.

This marvelous plant is really quite easy to grow outside. It actually grows in clumps and then spreads as well by seed. You'll find that in the winter, the stems of the plant will die off, but don't worry about that. They shoot up again on their own the following spring (don't you just love that?)

You can also start growing lemon balm simply by taking stem cuttings or, if you prefer, from seed. But I'm warning you, if the seeds find the right environment, you'll soon have lemon balm everywhere! Of course, there are worse things to have in your garden.

When you're planting the herb initially, the plants should be placed about 12 or 15 inches apart to give them plenty of "elbowroom."

8. St. John's Wort

Yes, *St. John's wort* is not native to the United States, but today you can find it growing along the roadside in many regions where the climate is mild. This prolific plant normally blooms from late May through September, depending on the climate.

In fact, its name comes to us because of the timing of its flowering. It once was believed that the plant blooms on June 24, the birthday of St. John the Baptist.

You probably are already familiar with this plant as a healing herb. Lately it has been not only recommended by just about everyone, but scrutinized closely by the medical community. Its best known healing trait is in the treatment of depression.

By all means, this is one of those perfect plants to try starting by seed. But if you're not up to that challenge, you can also propagate it through small cuttings or by rooting. No matter how you choose to start the plant, you'll eventually want to give them quite a bit of space so they don't crowd each other out. You can thin them when the seedlings are about two inches tall.

For optimum growing purposes it really doesn't matter where you plant this herb. It'll grow just about anywhere. It grows well in full to partial sun, but also tolerates the shade well. It grows best in moist light soils though.

9. Feverfew

Does the name not sound familiar? I'm sure the flower is. *Feverfew*, known for centuries as a natural cure for a migraine headache, has a flower that closely resembles the daisy. White petals with yellow centers, accent the green serrated leaves of this plant. If left to its own devices, these gorgeous flowers can grow to a height of nearly two feet.

In addition to migraines, many individuals say that using this plant has helped their arthritis and rheumatism.

And the most beautiful aspect of this amazing plant is that it'll bloom just about all summer long.

And it really isn't a fussy plant at all. Feverfew grows in just about any type of soil. This makes it the perfect plant to place between stones or pavers on your walkways and paths.

You should definitely try starting this plant from seeds. You'll probably have good luck with this method. If you're not quite brave enough, that's alright too. Feverfew will catch on and grow from cuttings just as well.

10. Valerian

Never considered this plant as part of your herbal garden? Perhaps you should give it a second look. Although the first year or two of growing these plants you're not even going to find one flower on them.

They won't be the most pleasantly fragrant herb in your garden either. But if you are a serious herbalist, you'll probably want to include this herb anyway.

Why? It appears to be a versatile healing herb. But you really don't have to take my word for it. Herbalists and other healers throughout the ages have been using this plant for a variety of illnesses and health conditions.

Valerian is said to be a great natural treatment for anxiety, as well as nervous tension and restlessness. It has also been said to help relieve stomach cramps and various digestive disorders. And that's just the start of what herbalists like about this plant.

Don't let its lack of flowers over the first several years deter you from growing this. Its foliage alone, without any blooms, will add texture and color to your garden.

The best method of starting your own plants is by separating the roots and then planting these separately. Another advantage to growing Valerian is that it really isn't particular about where it grows. It can grow almost anywhere.

If you've got a damp area in your garden where nothing else grows, try placing a couple plants there. Or if you have some rocky spots that look empty, valerian plants will fill those nicely too.

Chapter 3:

Design a Garden

> *Got your herbs all lined up in a row, ready to plant? Now it's time to design your garden. Whether it takes up your entire yard or just a small square, the more thought you put into it, the more beautiful it will be.*

What? You never thought of yourself as an "architect"? Go look into the mirror and introduce yourself to . . . well, you. You are about to be the architect and the creative vision behind your very own herb garden.

Don't worry, we'll take it slow. But, you're still taking an active hand in the designing of exactly where your garden goes. You'll be utterly amazed at just how easy it is.

Most people (and you might not be one of them) start their hobby on a modest scale. They begin by dedicating an area of about 20 by 4 feet to herbs. Then they break this area up into 12 by 18 inch plots with each different herb assigned its own special plot.

Just a quick hint and something to think about before you go shopping for these plants. Within this space, it's not unusual to see parsley and purple basil as border plants. These are usually not only placed in a spot that's handy to pick, but they're a colorful way to add beauty to this spot in your yard.

But I'm getting ahead of myself now because if you really want a well-designed garden, then you need to pick up a pencil and several pieces of graph paper. You're about to outline and literally design your very own herb garden.

It's really not nearly as frightening as it sounds. In fact, it's quite fun. After all, if Ralph Waldo Emerson is correct (and who am I to argue with a dead writer) then every thing we see in this world started as a thought and your herb garden is no different.

The best way to transfer a thought into a reality is to write it down. Let's face it, you know that your herb garden is blooming and growing wildly in your imagination already anyway.

> *"No two gardens are the same. No two days are the same in one garden." ~Hugh Johnson*

Long before any digging is done, you're planting the seeds of your garden as you visualize where your basil will live and whether you'll put your valerian in the left corner or in the middle of the garden.

And don't worry. You definitely don't have to be an artist to sketch a garden especially if you cheat just a little as I suggested earlier. Just use graph paper and this will help keep things in perspective for you.

> Before you start to sketch though, there's five **MUST-ASK** questions only you can answer. These questions have a direct bearing on the eventual look, feel and overall effect of your garden:
>
> **1. How large of a space do you have for your garden?**
>
> **2. How much sun does it get?** (Is it predominantly sunny or are there more total hours of shade?)
>
> **3. What growing zone are you in?** (You can find this out by going to: http://www.usna.usda.gov/Hardzone/ushzmap.html
>
> **4. How are you planning to spend time in your garden?** (How do you intend to use your garden?)
>
> **5. What type of soil do you have?**

Now that your ideal herb garden is beginning to gel in your mind, you can transfer those tentative ideas onto paper. And remember that you're creating this in paper and pencil, not casting it in stone.

What does that mean? It means that you're going to have an eraser right along side your paper because you're bound to change your mind at least once during this process.

To help keep you accurate, each square on your graph paper equals one foot in your eventual garden. This makes it super-simple to transfer the ideas into the physical world later.

In addition to this, you may also want to have some type of circular template so you can easily trace around it. Some plants, shrubs and even trees are usually drawn as various circles in a sketched garden design.

For example, let's say tucked among your herb garden you have a three foot wide dwarf shrub. You'll need a circle encompassing three squares on your graph paper.

Now, if you really want to nail down your imagination, you'll have some colored pencils lined up for your use as well. How else are you going to know what *color* herbs to place next to each other?

Planning Your Garden on Paper

Step #1

This exercise is valuable because it allows you to actually lay out and "try on" any number of garden plans. At a loss in where to start? Begin by showing what you already have in place; i.e. those things that just aren't going to move like full grown trees.

Other immovable structures you may have to work around include fences, backyard decks or patios.

Step #2

Next, decide which views you'd like to create. This means what the overall look of your garden will be. Included in this process is determining aspects about the area you'd like to "soften" up a bit or perhaps hide altogether.

Are you looking forward to sitting at your kitchen table, sipping that first cup of coffee in the morning to see echinacea blooming? Hawthorne growing? Even the purplish round chubby head of a chive bloom staring back at you?

Or do you prefer to sit there drinking your coffee, while at the same time you drink in the luscious scents of some aromatic herbs?

Now that you've taken that step, continue with what you'll see from your window or patio in all four seasons. Obviously in spring and summer, you'll be looking at foliage and blooms. But what do you want to see in autumn? Do you really want to look at nothing but worn out flowers?

Step #3

Draw the lines that are to be borders of your planting areas. Remember that each square represents one foot. Keep a 12-inch ruler next to you as a visual reminder if you have to. Leave room for the layering of different types of herbs, like your perennials and your shrubs.

Step #4

Now it's time to give serious consideration to the types of herbs you'd like to have and where you'd like to place them. You must be precise about this. Start with perennial herbs and then try to keep these in groups of around three to five plants in an area. You'll appreciate this piece of advice once they've bloomed.

This is the fun part of the design process, the part where your seeds of imagination really can germinate into a beautiful and fragrant herb garden.

Ideas for Your Garden

Don't tell me you're sitting there without a clue of what to choose. Allow me to give you a helpful hint or two.

Firstly, flip through some gardening magazines. Even though you may not have a backyard like they're showing, what is it about those gardens that are especially appealing to you? What keeps drawing you back to this garden? Jot it down. Now look at a few other magazines. Go to your local library or visit a bookstore in search of magazines.

Secondly, you can check out some websites. Here you'll get a wide variety of ideas of what to place in your garden, depending on your purpose for planting.

Types of Herb Gardens

Until I gained an interest in herbs, I really had no idea that there were different categories of herb garden designs. But I quickly learned differently. You can find entire books devoted to the exact design and layout of gardens including plant placement and sometimes even detailed explanations.

I would be remiss if I didn't mention them to you. But don't feel that just because you're starting a new hobby that you have to redesign your entire backyard. Not unless you really wanted a good excuse to.

Much of the design of your garden, in fact, depends on the amount of shade your yard receives, the amount of available sun, the type of soil you have and the kinds of herbs you'd like to grow.

But, still it's interesting and fun to learn more about the design of various gardens and their origins.

Formal Gardens

The layouts of formal gardens actually date back to Medieval and Renaissance Europe. If you visit public botanical gardens you'll discover that even today, we're still influenced by these practices.

Of course, we don't know what average Joe "Serf" and his family planted or how they planted them. No doubt they were arranged in an order that emphasized usefulness and ease of access.

But we do know that monasteries, royal palaces and the gardens of the upper classes were more defined and followed certain ideas.

In fact, one of the oldest renditions of a formal herb garden that is known dates back to the ninth century. As far as historians know, the garden, which was designed for a Benedictine monastery was never actually constructed.

But the logic behind the plans is amazing. First, the plans include a large, rectangular kitchen garden. Some 18 beds of vegetables and herbs were anticipated.

Another 16 beds were to be devoted strictly to the medicinal herbs. And the anticipated location was quite interesting – right next to the doctor's house near the infirmary.

Both of these garden plots were to be walled; each were to be laid out in two parallel rows of rectangular raised bed and each bed was devoted to a single species of herbs. Yes indeed, the monks knew exactly what they wanted.

This was a basic utilitarian design and is quite typical of mastic life as well as just about any large medieval garden.

Fast-forward some 600 years later. We have drawings of 15th century gardens of rural manors and townhouses. What we know about these was composed of any number of small square or rectangular beds arranged in simple grid pattern. Paths, with ample room for strolling, connected the various squares.

We still use this general outline to this day. It's not a bad basic design for an herb garden and you might even want to consider it. After all, its design is based on ease of use. This design, species by species, makes it easy to harvest the medicinal herbs as well as rotate the short-lived crops of salad herbs.

Indeed, this particular design of a formal garden works not only on a visually pleasing level, but also on the utilitarian level.

Medieval Gardens

But don't think that every garden in that era was laid out exactly like that as many were not. A lot of residents of these vast estates tossed utility out the door and followed their own imaginations.

One gentleman created a garden that featured the lawn in the center of the yard, and surrounding this in a circular fashion, he planted sweet-smelling herbs like basil, rue, and sage. These gardens promoted elements that many of us still promote today when we grow our herb gardens; elements such as intimacy, enclosure and fragrance.

The Botanical Garden

These originated in the Medieval era as well. You might be surprised to learn the original intent was a teaching tool. Created by universities to teach their students medicine, these gardens included narrow, rectangular beds much in the Medieval fashion. Take for example the *Chelsea Physic Garden* in London. Founded by the London Society of Apothecaries in the 17th century, the garden beds are still being used today in the original Medieval design.

Medieval Gives Rise to Renaissance

Ah, the Renaissance, known for a resurgence of . . . well, it looks like just about everything. Art wasn't the only item to gain sudden popularity. The herb garden changed form during this timeframe as well.

It went well beyond the basic forms of the Medieval version and grew into more complex endeavors. It's as if those who witnessed the unfolding of the art world weren't satisfied to contain the changes to just one area.

Suddenly gone were the neat, rectangular designs that emphasized utility. Now, gardeners designed for beauty. The patterns of herbs grew more complex.

A design called "the knot" was developed which is still used today in herb gardens. This featured decorative interlacing bands of neatly clipped herbs. A geometric design within a square, rectangle or even a circle was created on the ground.

Each figure in the pattern was then assigned and filled with a single herb, meticulously manicured to maintain the ultimate design.

If spaces were found between these clipped outlines, they were filled with gravel or different colored sand. In the Elizabethan era, these gaps were filed with lavender, germander or even santolina.

The knot garden to this day is still one of the most popular designs. Open just about any book devoted exclusively to garden design and its one of the first designs you'll see.

Devising Your Culinary Herb Garden

"But I don't want to create a huge garden just for herbs," you might be thinking. And that's quite understandable. Thankfully there's really no need to. Why dedicate your time and effort to a process of designing and planting a garden that you really won't enjoy. You see, herb growing is all about enjoyment.

So, let me clue you in on a little secret. Herbs (culinary herbs especially) can make themselves at home just about anyplace in your existing flower garden. Even if you don't have a flower garden now, you can find some place in your yard for an herb here and there. That's just part of the beauty and ease of growing herbs.

Got roses blooming already? Go ahead and place an herb as its neighbor. You may want to place your basil next to those petunias. It's your garden, so why not? If you already have a small vegetable garden going, by all means intersperse your vegetables with herbs.

And don't panic if you've never planted anything before. I know one gentleman who planted catnip along the cement block foundation of his back porch. He wasn't into planting a lot, just four or five plants. The green added wonderful color and his cat appreciated and enjoyed them.

You get the point. Design is great, if you enjoy doing it. But if you're just testing the waters, you may not want to devote that much time to it.

But if you want to go for a larger look but keep it informal, start with the herbs that you know are going to grow taller than the others. These specific ones are sure to add interest to the landscape you're laying out. Most of these you'll want to place behind the shorter ones.

In a very real sense, your completed garden will look layered. The shortest plants will be in front, some of them being used as border accents. Choose the plants proportionally to place behind the others. You'll want to see all of them and certainly you'll want your visitors to as well. What use would it do to have the parsley hidden behind a larger coriander plant?

You'll be surprised at just how many of the herbs will grow quite large if you allow them and encourage them. Bay laurel, by nature is a large herb. You can encourage this plant to grow a larger trunk, simply by pruning it.

Or you may just let it grow into its natural shape (which has many larger main stems) simply by doing nothing.

Rosemary, which is normally not a very large plant, can be encouraged to grow bigger. All you need to do is remove its lower branches. You can also allow your garden sage to rise above the rest.

> *"The greatest gift of the garden is the restoration of the five senses".* ~Hanna Rio

The look still isn't quite what you had in mind? Why not plant certain herbs in their own containers, and then place these in your herb garden. Containers create a pleasing texture to the eye. Not only that, but depending on the type of container and its color, adding a delightful dash of color to your garden.

The only piece of advice I'd like to give you before you begin is this: place this culinary garden as close to the kitchen as possible. This way your favorite herbs are nearby, not only ready to use but easy to get to. Instead of reaching for the store-bought bottles of dried herbs, you simply step outside your back door and pick a few fresh ones. Does life really get any better than this?

Another piece of advice for gardening with herbs: don't be stingy, be generous when you plant. Don't plant just one basil plant or one thyme. Plant species in groups of three or even five.

Other ideas to keep in mind when you're planting your informal culinary garden include the presence of a path through part of it. This path not only serves as a wonderful meditation road (for those of who you are "thoughtful") but it also serves the larger purpose of providing easy access to all the herbs without trampling through the smaller ones.

Now I'll Drink To That!

Really don't want to deal with a lot of digging? Or perhaps your backyard isn't quite big enough?

Why not confine your culinary herb garden to just one or two "whiskey" barrels?

That's right. Two of these containers hold enough herbs to easily supply a family of two or three with the essentials.

What a tremendously attractive addition to your yard or deck these containers would be.

Accents in Your Garden

Your culinary garden doesn't need to be large, but consider placing certain accents in it nonetheless. A bay tree itself can be an accent, or you may want to add a sundial, a fountain or even a sculpture (as a nod to herb gardens of old) to add interest.

And just because it's informal and small doesn't mean it's without some type of structure. Think of the borders of your garden. You'll want something that grows low. And you'll probably want to keep it looking somewhat uniform. So you don't want to put only three or five different plants along the border.

Maintain a constant border with one herb, perhaps a row of parsley. You'd be surprised at how this pulls the entire concept of your garden together. If you want to use two or maybe even three plants as a border, arrange them in a way that you have a visually pleasing pattern to them.

Grouping Your Plants

When deciding exactly where your specific herbs will live, you really don't have to worry about breaking any hard and fast gardener's rules. But it might help you if you separated the herbs that like dry soil, like rosemary and thyme, from those that need more moisture, such as basil and parsley.

Of course, you should place the herbs that you use most frequently as close to your kitchen door as possible. As much as we're aiming for beauty in the garden, the ultimate goal of this culinary herb garden is to enhance your cooking. If the garden isn't functional, then it's just not successful, no matter how beautiful it is.

Your Private Tea Garden

A garden dedicated to the growing of herbs just for tea is not a new idea. And when the weather is nice, the garden is not only a source of your tea, but it can be the setting to leisurely sip your tea and meditate. It may also be the place to serve this fine beverage to your guests.

Let your imagination rule when it comes to the design of this specific garden. You can use any shape or configuration from an informal and cottage plan to a more formal approach or even a Zen like creation.

It's not unusual to walk into a backyard only to discover the tea garden that was created is in the shape of a teapot. Some individuals shape their gardens like teacups, complete with saucers.

Consider this fun idea: a teapot shaped garden, about eight to ten feet from the lid to the bottom of the "pot." The size from the "handle" on one end to the "spout" on the other end would be about 10 to 12 feet. This size is large enough to contain 15 to 20 plants, all generously spaced.

Your only real limitation with this design is the sunlight available and of course, if your yard can accommodate such a design. Just bear in mind (and I know this seems obvious), that the larger the garden, the more maintenance it demands.

When creating your tea garden, no matter what shape you ultimately decide it'll be, keep in mind that historically these types of gardens have been places for reflection and relaxation. You can create an additional sense of calm by generating a feeling of enclosure within this space.

Use hedges, trellises or even wooden fences to set this space apart. If you don't want to use these types of items, you could also enclose using rows of potted plants.

What is a tea garden without a tea table and a set of chairs or at least benches? Sit here alone, with family or a close friend to enjoy a cup of tea made from your own fresh herbs.

Accent Your Garden with Tea-Related "Accessories"

Now here's a cute idea. Why not edge your garden bed with some old teaspoons or even mismatched saucers turned on end. You may even want to attach old teacups to garden stakes to use as plant markers.

Why not take your garden to the next level with accessorizing? Buy a few used teapots at yard sales, swap meets, or thrift stores. Plant a few herbs in these to display in your garden. You can also plant a few herbs in a setting of teacups as well.

Beyond that, you can use teacups as bird baths as well. Actually if you set your imagination free, there's no end to how you can decorate your tea garden.

Whether you pay any attention to the design of your garden to create an elaborate back yard theme, or you decide to just grow a few functional herbs from your windowsill, you'll be taking that first exciting step to "communing" with nature as you've never known it before.

The aromatic fragrances of herbs are not only enticing, they're downright mesmerizing. Add to that the beauty of some of the most stunning flowers Mother Nature ever made and this easily becomes one addictive hobby.

Now let's get down to the real business of herb gardening: the herbs themselves.

Chapter 4:

Outdoor Gardening

> *In a nutshell, here's what it takes to grow healthy herbs outside. The right soil, just enough water (but not too much), and protection from the cold, winter months. Plus one more thing: companion plants would help. Find out about all of these aspects of growing your herbs outdoors in this chapter.*

It's one of those no-brainers. Healthy, vigorous herbs sprout from healthy, nutritious soil. Good soil is the basis of plants that are resistant to insect pests and various diseases. The pleasant surprise is that creating a healthy base for your herbs is incredibly easy.

Whether you're growing culinary, medicinal or tea herbs, they all need the same basic soil: three parts of garden soil, one part peat, compost or aged manure and one part sand. It's that easy. Give your herbs this and you're well on your way to producing healthy, strong herbs.

Beyond that, you'll notice that many herb guides advise the soil be "well drained." It's just a fact of herbal life; these plants hate wet soil. You may be wondering how to ensure that the soil in your yard is well drained.

To create this ideal growing condition, simply place a three-inch layer of compressed stone into your soil about 15 to 18 inches under the surface. Return the soil, blended with compost and sand, on top of these stones. Be sure in doing this, that you fill this top soil just a little higher than it was originally. This allows for some settling of the soil as time passes.

As an additional insurance policy, you may also want to purchase a soil-moisture meter. Because this device actually measures the moisture at the roots of the plant, this can eliminate a lot of the guess work that's usually involved in estimating moisture.

Planting Your Herbs

If you're planting or even transplanting seedlings outside, the best method I've found is to dig the hole, adding just a "dash" of compost and bone meal for drainage as well as extra nutrients.

You'll discover as you grow a larger variety of herbs that many herbs grow best in an alkaline soil. Knowing this, you may want to add a tablespoon or two of agricultural lime. This helps the roots to absorb nutrients more efficiently. All of this gets mixed into the soil in the hole before putting the herb in.

You'll discover too that even though your herbs are eventually destined to be part of an outdoor garden, you'll want to start them indoors. Some herbs just seem to get a much healthier start when begun inside. Some of the plants you may want to start inside include basil, borage, marjoram, oregano, chamomile, catnip, sorrel and thyme.

Simply place the seeds in flats containing well-drained, airy soil with lots of organic matter. You'll find that borage and sorrel prefer to be in soil that is moist and rich.

When your seedlings are about four inches tall and the weather is warm, you're ready to "introduce" them to the outside environment. As strange as this may sound, it is very necessary. It's a step many beginning gardeners fail to do, simply because they don't know about it.

Introducing these plants gradually to the outdoors is called *hardening off*. This process should not begin in earnest until the overnight temperatures rise to a dependable 50 degrees or more.

Also, ensure that the plants you're hardening off are placed in sturdy containers with moist soil. Start the process simply by placing the flats outside starting at 9 a.m. Leave them here for several hours.

Remember that you are dealing with delicate seedlings. Don't take them out on windy days. These plants are small so even a light gust may blow the pots off the deck or patio.

> *"Gardening is a matter of your enthusiasm holding up until your back gets used to it." ~Author Unknown*

The potential for broken stems in this situation is extremely real. If any of your plants have any lids or cellophane coverings, make sure you remove them before you take them out. On the first day be especially vigilant that the soil doesn't dry out or the leaves don't droop.

Repeat this process for the next five or six days. Every day increase the amount of time the seedlings spend outdoors. The only exception to this is the unexpected, wild fluctuations of temperature that sometimes happens during the spring.

If the temperature varies more than 15 degrees from one day to the next in either direction then shorten the seedlings

exposure outside. Basically, what you're doing is acclimatizing your plants to the environment.
Don't place the herbs out if it is extremely rainy or excessively hot. The process won't be ruined when they're kept in for a day or so.

Do this for about five days. After that your plants should be ready to be planted outdoors.

Alternatives to Hardening Off

Some herbalists prefer to use other methods than the hardening off to process to prepare the seedlings for the outdoor garden. One method is a low-water approach.

In this method, you don't place the plants outside, you leave them indoors, but you decrease the watering of them in increments. Each time, allow the soil to dry out a little more than the last time. Do this for two to three weeks.

Eventually you'll only water them when they begin to droop. Once they're to this point, they're ready for the outside world.

Fertilizing Your Herbs

You may think the fastest and easiest way to obtain healthy plants is to fertilize them. This is certainly true, but to an extent. Just as with everything else in this world, moderation is the key in nourishing your plants.

You may be surprised to learn that this is a point of diminishing returns when it comes to fertilizing herbs. Herbs grown in overly fertilized soil actually grow poorly.

Your herbs aren't completely maintenance free. They require regular care and attention, just like flowers or vegetable plants. After the initial planting of the herbs, continue to apply compost or fertilizer to them on a regular basis.

You may also want to add mulch occasionally as well. Mulch helps to preserve moisture. It also prevents weeds from overtaking your garden.

Growing Herbs in Containers

Many herb growers are concerned with the plants they grow in containers. One of the questions I receive most often is: "How can you be certain your container herb is well drained?" It really isn't as hard as it seems.

When you initially buy your container for your plants, be sure the container already has drain holes in it. The better containers will have them. If you decide to decorate by planting your herbs in unconventional containers, a teapot for example, then create several holes In the bottom to ensure proper drainage

These holes don't need to be large. But to ease your worry that the soil will leak through these holes, fill the bottom of the container with gravel or stones. That way you'll be sure that the soil won't escape.

If you're planning on growing these herbs indoors, keep a waterproof tray underneath your pots. But be careful not to water these plants too much.

Specific Soil for Certain Herbs

Of course, one soil doesn't necessarily work for all herbs. By necessity, there are different needs for different plants. And this is where the expertise of your local nursery is indispensable. They'll know exactly what type of soil your particular herbs will need.

Watering Your Herbs

Here's a good rule of thumb that I've finally found works for me. When the natural rainfall is less than one inch within the week, water your herbs.

And don't forget that one of the great uses for mulch is as an effective control mechanism. When you go to the nursery to buy your mulch, you'll have a variety from which to choose.

Consider buying the bark chips or the shredded bark. Other good mulches you might consider include compost, ground corncobs, pecan hulls or even dried grass clippings.

When you spread your mulch, don't be stingy. You need to spread enough that it has half a chance of performing the job you want it to. That means you want it at least three inches deep.

Diseases, Insects and Other Pests

Herbs grown outdoors which have access to ample air circulation, sunlight and water drainage are seldom affected with either disease or damage by insects.

The usual suspects that attack herbs, such as mites and aphids, are held in check by natural predators and parasites. And this is especially true if you're growing a wide variety of different herbs. Of course, you don't want to use chemical insecticides.

Instead, search out insecticidal soap as well as horticultural oil. These can help fight any attacks as well as keeping your plants chemical free. If you have troubles with some of the larger pests, like beetles and caterpillars, simply pick them off.

Companion Plants

When it comes to herbs, companion plants may prove to be a vital key in the overall health of your garden, not only your herb garden, but your patch of vegetables and flower bed too.

That's because some plants actually grow better when they're sitting next to other plants. It might not sound very sensible at first, but the concept is really quite simple.

If you start to add specific herbs to your vegetable or flower garden you may notice a decidedly improved level of overall health for all the plants, depending on the herbs you've put there.

Let me give you a classic example of this. When white settlers came to North America, they soon learned that the Native Americans had what they referred to as the "three Sisters" which was a combination of corns, beans and squash. Now if you learned this in school or elsewhere as I did, you might have assumed these three plants were "sisters" because they were a vital part of their overall diet.

But here's the rest of the story. When planted together, they actually help the others to grow. First of all, the beans are the "nitrogen-fixers" for the other plants and climb the stalks of the corn. The squash shades the ground for the sake of the health of the other two plants holding the moisture longer in the ground.

More Examples of Companion Plants

Now here's an example that might have come straight from your garden: garlic and roses. As much as it might sound like a new heavy metal rock band, it's really how lots of gardeners arrange their plants. Garlic and roses are companion plants.

The pungent scent of the garlic repels a portion of the rose plant's worst pests, the aphids. To a gardener who's trying hard to stay organic, this is quite exciting information.

But you can also have the opposite affect. Some plants just don't grow well at all when placed together. For example Irish potatoes don't grow well at all when placed next to turnips or pumpkins.

There's actually a very good reasons for these companion plants, or in this case, non-companion plants. Tall plants may block the sun from lower lying sun-loving plants. Others may actually create some negative biochemical reaction with those around them.

Here are a few other herbs you may want to consider planting with others, as well as some you may want to keep these herbs from being next to.

Basil. This plant loves tomatoes and you can bet it's a mutual admiration club. In fact they are so good together some gardeners have developed a rule of (green) thumb: three basil plants for every tomato plant.

But here's one more thing you may not have known about basil: it actually repels flies and mosquitoes.

Borage. This particular herb encourages the growth of strawberries. It's also a great companion plant for tomatoes and squash.

Chamomile. Be sure to plant these with your onions and cabbage and watch all three of them grow strong and healthy.

Chives. Did you know that if you steeped chives in water, it's a great organic method of killing powdery mildew disease? When you plant it, make sure it's near your carrots if you have a vegetable garden as well as any apple trees you may have on your property.

Dill. Dill appreciates being near cabbage, cucumbers, corn and lettuce. One hint: don't plant dill near fennel just to avoid cross pollination.

Garlic. Of course, we've already mentioned how this plant loves tomatoes, but go ahead and plant it near fruit trees as well. Garlic repels the red spider mites. And this herb, steeped in water is another effective insecticide.

Lemon balm. Plant this plant with the tomatoes.

Mint. Will help your cabbage grow, but don't let it get near your parsley.

Oregano. Think collard, broccoli, cauliflower, cabbage. Plant the oregano plant with these.

Parsley. You'll make your parsley and your tomato plants both happy if you planted them together. You can also plant parsley with chives, carrots and asparagus. But keep the parsley away from the mint.

Rosemary. Keep this away from the potatoes. But, you'll want to plant this herb near cabbage, carrots, beans and sage.

Sage. In addition to rosemary, sage also encourages the growth and health of carrots and cabbage. But please keep it away from your cucumber.

Thyme. Cabbage appreciates being near thyme. This herb repels worms that love to munch on the cabbage.

Now that you know how to keep your outside herbs healthy and happy, let's see what it takes to maintain quality herbs inside your home. That's the focus of the next chapter.

> *"Don't wear perfume in the garden - unless you want to be pollinated by bees.". ~Anne Raver*

Chapter 5:

Indoor Gardening

> *While growing herbs indoors is very handy, it does largely depend on a delicate balance of soil, water and light. Discover just how crucial these three elements are.*

Gardening outdoors is great, but if it's a bit more than you're willing to handle right now, then perhaps you should consider confining your initial foray into herbs to indoors.

Actually, there are some advantages to this, not the least of which is growing a small group of herbs and maintaining their health. Your taste buds and the herbs will thank you, and your back will be grateful as well.

Perhaps you would rather start small as countless people do. Many discover their love of herbs after they've grown several merely for practical purposes, never suspecting they would end up with a life-long love of the plants.

If that's the case, your kitchen herb garden may very well take the form of a window box full of plants or perhaps just a group of planters in your kitchen. However, just because it's small, doesn't mean it should be thrown together without some basic forethought.

Using Light

There's really only one catch to growing herbs, especially in the initial stages. These plants crave and really do need ten to 12 hours of sunlight every day to thrive. And herbs prefer natural to artificial light, hands down.

Before you make your final decision on which herbs to grow, take a good look at the sunlight that comes through your kitchen windows. This ultimately dictates which herbs you *can* grow. Got a southern or a western exposure? This means you've got a sunny, hot climate.

If your windowsills aren't wide enough to place containers on them, consider extending the sills. You don't have to be a carpenter to do this. You can easily add a finished one by attaching a six-inch board to the windowsill. You can easily secure it simply by screwing it into the existing window sill board.

Or you may want to consider purchasing one of the windowsill extenders that cat lovers use to ensure their felines have a nice view of the outdoors. You should be able to get several plants on one of these.

But if you don't want to do that, simply put shelving up in front of the window.

The only step left is to figure out is which specific windows face which direction. This you'll need to know as an avid indoor gardener. Those windows on the south side of your home, for instance, are privy to the longest lasting and the brightest light.

This also means that this is the hottest portion of your home. But that doesn't mean every herb will want to live there. The plants that are more tender may burn with that much light.

More indirect light and much less heat comes through the windows on the north side of your house. Light on the other two sides (the east and west) offer bright light, but nothing that can compete with that southern exposure. If you must put some flowers either in the west or east windows, choose west first. This direction will be warmer than the windows facing east.

Also you should turn your plants once a week or so to allow the sunlight to reach all sides of the plant.

Artificial Light

If you can't give your plants that much light even on your best windows, then perhaps you should invest in a *grow light*. This form of lighting is relatively inexpensive and you can find them at just about any nursery or discount stores and even hardware stores.

You'll want the artificial lights to be about 10 inches above the young herb starters plants. For more mature or larger herbs, hang them about a foot to a foot and a half above the plants.

You'll need to keep these lights on the plants about 10 hours a day. This simulates the time the sun would be shining on them.

Types of Light

If you talk to any three cultivators of indoor herbs, you're very likely to receive three very distinct and opinionated ideas when it comes to what kind of light to place above your herbs. You have basically two choices: fluorescent and high-intensity discharge light.

Let's talk about fluorescent lighting first. This kind is the most recognizable to us as you see them everywhere. They're usually long and thin. Believe it or not, home gardeners have used this specific type of lighting for years. It's especially useful for starting seeds. But it's also good for encouraging growth in plants as well.

The intensity of the fluorescent light is low, so they are ideal for encouraging the growth of seedlings. But they are also ideal for low-growing herbs.

Consider this: a standard four-foot unit with two 40-watt bulbs (or tubes) illuminates an area of about eight inches in width.

But more than that, you can also buy specialty tubes for your specific needs. These array of tubes are available depending on the needs of your herbs.

But don't overlook a combination of the standard cool and warm white tubes as these are effective as well. *Verilux* tubes are another choice. Experts say this type of light is the closest approximation to the sun. These lights cost about $10 each.

On the other hand, a brand called *Vita-Lite,* is labeled as a "power twist" tube. It produces somewhat more light per watt than the standard fluorescent bulb does. And the quality of this light is well balanced for optimum plant growth. But the cost may be intimidating for you: $18 each.

The brightness of light is measured either in lumens or as foot candles. Lumens is a reference to the amount of light available at the source. Foot candles measures the amount of light falling on the area.

As you move farther from the light, then, the lumens would naturally stay the same. However, as you can imagine, the farther you travel from the light, the amount of foot candles decreases.

A bright but overcast day measures about 1,000 foot candles. By contrast, a bright sunshiny day generates about 10,000 foot candles.

Contrast this to fluorescent lights. At six inches from the source, you'll be receiving about 700 foot candles. When you're a foot from the light, the foot candle measurement drops to 450.

A Note on Hydroponic Gardening…

Many gardeners are beginning to switch to hydroponic gardening for many different reasons. These types of gardens are small and can easily be grown inside and are perfect for most vegetables and herbs. Also the equipment required for hydroponic gardening is not expensive and are relatively easy to manage.

Hydroponic gardening is the growing of plants without soil, in other words, "dirt less gardening". There are many methods of hydroponic gardening, most of which work better than regular soil gardening because it is easier to give the plant exactly what it needs when it needs it. Plants will only receive what you give them; therefore you will be able to regulate the pH, nutrients, nutrient strength, water amount, and light amount.

Humidity

The ultimate dry environment of your house may present another problem in growing your plants indoors. If your house doesn't have a whole-house humidifier, you can still provide the perfect humidity for these plants and not break the bank.

First, remember to finely mist the plants with water weekly. You can also add humidity to the specific area where the plants are located simply by setting a dish of water near the heat source in the room. As the heat source operates, it naturally evaporates the water, which in turn adds moisture into the air.

Another good way to moisturize the plants is to fill trays with pea gravel. Then pour water into these trays so the water fills about half the tray. Now simply set the plants on top of the gravel.

Any one of these (or using all three of these in extreme measures) should solve even the toughest of the humidity problems.

Watering

Herbs grown in containers tend to dry out more quickly than those grown outside. But don't worry; it's easy enough to check the status. Simply stick a finger into the soil. Make sure you get at least get half an inch below the surface to feel the moisture.

If the soil feels dry to the touch, then you'll need to water the plant. As much as you may be tempted, don't over-water these indoor herbs. You'll only be promoting root rot as well as the development of a disease called powdery mildew.

This plant disease is probably one of the most recognizable. If your herb is afflicted with this, it will look as if it has powdery splotches of white or gray on not only the leaves, but also on its stems.

While this disease is not fatal, it does indeed stress the plant. In fact, repeated infections will weaken the plant. And if the mildew is not corrected, it may cover so much of the plant it eventually cripples the plants ability to go through photosynthesis.

Powdery Mildew

Should one of your herbs become infected with powdery mildew, caring for it is much easier than you may think. Your first move of course is to remove and destroy all areas that are infected.

You'll then want to improve the circulation of your plants. You do this by thinning your plants out and pruning the affected plants.

Don't fertilize it while the herb is infected,. You may find that a bit contradictory because I've just said this mildew weakens the plant. But the disease thrives on young, succulent growth. So while you and your herb are actually battling this problem, refrain from fertilizing it.

Another tip to help discourage the mildew is to not water the plants from above. When you water the plants, move the lowest branches around in order to pour the water straight on the soil itself. You really don't want to get the stems wet.

You may be forced eventually to apply a fungicide to some of your herbs. That doesn't mean you're using harsh chemicals. That would certainly negate some of the reasons for growing these specific plants at home.

The fungicide you'll be applying (and you can simply ask any nursery about this) is created from such natural ingredients as potassium bicarbonate, sulfur or even copper.

The Actual Planting

It's about time, you're probably thinking. But, it's important to know what to do with your plants. Now you'll learn how to plant them properly. Taking care of them during the growing season will be easier than you may have imagined when you first started.

Believe it or not, you're pretty well set already. If you're starting with nothing (as many first-time gardeners are) you'll want to ensure that you have a good supply of six-inch planting pots. This is probably the best size herb pot.

You can grow many seeds or small bulbs in just one of these pots (adhering to the "one-inch" apart" dogma.) You'll recall that all bulbs need to be at least one inch apart in order to grow healthy.

Before you place any kind of soil or combination of media into these pots, line them with stones and bark chips. This serves as your drainage system as well as an effective aeration mechanism.

When you fill these pots with soil, don't use just any variety. Herbs are a bit in the "snobbish" range when it comes to soil. Use a good quality soil. It should be loose as well as containing as many of the nutrients as possible that your plants will need.

Bury these seeds or small bulbs in the pots about an inch apart across the entire surface of the container.

If, on the other hand, you're transplanting nursery-bought seedlings, you have two choices. First, you can remove these plants from their original containers, placing them in the holes you've dug into the potting soil. The other option is to plant them and their containers in the potting soil together.

While this second selection may sound a bit off the wall, it has a definite advantage. When you plant the container with the herb, you are assured that the plant has its root systems intact and undamaged. It also just happens to make growing and transplanting several herbs much quicker and easier.

A plant can grow in the same pot for one season. However it's easy to recognize when your herbs have outgrown their homes.

The telltale sign is that the roots start to burst out of the bottom of the container.

"Yes, It Really Is Alright To Pamper Your Herbs . . ."

And one of the best ways of pampering them is by providing these wonderful plants with proper ventilation.

My recommendation is to place a small, oscillating fan near the pots. This encourages the optimum distribution of air particles as well as the perfect degree of humidity.

Your plants will thank you with tastier and more potent herbs.

Chapter 6:

Caring for the Herbs

> *Once you get your plants growing, you'll no doubt want to somehow keep them from year to year. This chapter shows you how. This chapter also gives you some tips on harvesting and preserving your herbs for the "off season".*

As lovely as the growing season is, all good things must come to an end. As fall starts approaching, now is a good time to start planning for the winter.

This is the time to spring into action, harvesting the herbs you have and preserving them for the long winter. Then transplanting those you can to keep them growing next year as well.

It may sound like work, but keep in mind that these herbs have provided you with an incredible amount of joy throughout the spring and summer. They're about to provide you with more flavorful meals during the cold winter months. And some of these herbs may just help you avoid some of the toughest germs, and colds going around this winter.

Besides, as I'm sure you've figured out by now, this really isn't work, it's a labor of love.

Surviving a Cold, Hard Winter

While it might not seem like a "Valley-Forge Experience" to you, the winter months may prove hard on your plants. You may want to take a bit of extra care when it comes to their winter protection and survival.

Granted, many perennial herbs are quite hardy. They survive the winter quite well. But depending on the other types of herbs you've planted outside and where you happen to live, you may have to supply your plants with a little extra protection.

This is especially true if you live in any of the Midwestern or northern states. But there are plenty of other cold states from which to choose.

But more than just the cold, more herbs are killed by extreme and wild fluctuations in temperature rather than just the extreme cold.

To make sure your herbs see it through to another summer, what you do throughout the growing season plays a vital role. I know I'm sounding like a broken record, but there's a reason I keep returning to the theme of "well-drained" soil. It's just another layer of protection for your plants during the long, cold winter.

Herbs are especially subjected to "root rot" over the winter if the soil they're sitting in isn't well-drained. If you haven't taken much stock in "lightening up" your soil throughout the summer months, you should make it a priority in the fall. It's the best way to help ensure herb survival in the winter.

Pruning should only take place in the spring and summer months. Once fall appears, then you can gradually taper back on your pruning. You really want to encourage a little more growth in the fall as it helps to insulate the plants for the upcoming cold weather.

Also, consider protecting your herbs with an extra layer of mulch. Top the existing mulch off with evergreen branches or even some other material. Try not to use mulch that packs heavily down. It will only retain the moisture during the winter which very well may contribute to root rot.

Do you have herbs that you feel are marginally hardy such as rosemary or Greek oregano? If you have doubts about their ability to survive the winter, don't be afraid to dig them up, pot them and bring them inside for the winter. Once spring hits, they can be planted outside again.

Propagating New Plants

You've planted your herbs and they all seem to be doing quite nicely. But now, you'd really like to take that next step by propagating new plants.

There are three main methods to do this. You can:

1. Create more plants through dividing the roots of the existing plants,
2. Take cuttings of the herbs in your gardens
3. Through a method called "healing in" or "layering".

1. Root Division

This is a simple approach to creating more herbs. With a spade or shovel, work the roots from a clump of the densely growing herbs. Take this grouping out of the ground and separate the plants, starting at the roots. You want to do this rather carefully.

Once separated, you can place one of the groupings back in the original spot. The other group(s) may be planted anywhere you like.

2. Creating Herbs from Cuttings

This is another straightforward approach to propagating herbs. In either the spring or fall, you'll take a long, woody shoot from the plant of your choosing. Cut the shoot at an angle close the grand.

Remove the leaves from the very bottom of this cutting. Coating it with a rooting powder, you'll pot it in a light soil mix. Water this well.

3. Creating New Herbs Through Layering

Bend a long woody shoot and bury the middle of the stem under a few inches of soil. Hold it down with a small rock. Within a month to six weeks, the cutting or the healed-in stem develops its own root system. It's at this time that it's ready to be transplanted.

Harvesting, Preserving Herbs

Growing herbs is just part of the fun of keeping your herb garden. Another aspect of herb gardening which many people enjoy is the harvesting and the preserving of the herbs once the growing season ends.

Ask five different herb gardeners and you're bound to get five different ideas about the best method to harvest these plants. The great herbalist and nun of the 12th Century, Hildegard of Bingen firmly believed that all medicinal plants should be harvested when the moon was waxing, just prior to it becoming full. Herbs taken at this time, she believed, possessed their greatest potency.

She did concede, though, that the herbs would be preserved for an extended period of time if they were harvested during the waning of the moon.

Many herbalists have other ideas though. Many believe, for instance, that herbs should be gathered only during a full moon. This is the time, they contend, when the sap of the plants and the strength of their oils are the greatest.

While you may consider these ideas "old wives' tales" they do seem to have some validity. The seasons of harvesting seem to play a part in the potency.

Herbs whose medicinal active ingredients are found in their roots and rhizomes such as ginger, ginseng and mandrake for example, are more potent when harvested early in the spring or in late autumn. At this time, they have actually reserved much of their energy and essence below the ground.

In harvesting these types of herbs, dig widely around the plants, in order not to cut or damage the root system. Wash the roots with cold water and thoroughly dry them.

It's also true the essence of a plant becomes concentrated with each succeeding night. The herbs, therefore, are most potent when they're picked in the early hours of the morning well before the sun's heat and the light actually dissipate any essential oils in them.

And it's best to harvest the herbs on a morning that is clear and dry, just after the dew has evaporated from the leaves. Just about all herbs should be harvesting before they bloom.

The active healing substances of these plants also lose their potency after the flowering process, for obvious reasons. They've just spent much of their energy on actually blooming and generating seeds.

When you do harvest herbs, be sure to use sharp pruning clippers. You don't want to tear the stems. If you don't cut too low on the stem, you'll discover that some herbs, Basil is particularly noted for this, will produce more growth for the harvest.

As a part of keeping your garden growing, you may decide to deliberately *not harvest* several plants of various species. You may decide to allow them to seed towards the growth of next year's garden.

It's easy enough to collect these seeds. Choose the specific, individual plants which will go to seed. Just before the seeds have matured, place a paper bag, upside down, over each flower. Tie the mouth of the mouth of the bag with string or twine.

When the seeds have matured, cut off each seed head with the bag attached. Turn the bag right side up, tap the seeds into the bag and then remove the string and the plant.

Preserving Your Herbs

I have to admit, my initial idea of preserving herbs was taking a bottle of ginseng and placing it in a cool, dry place, just like the label instructed. I soon discovered fresh herbs don't work that way.

What I did learn is that preserving and storing fresh herbs is every bit as fun and rewarding as growing them. And this is especially true when it comes to medicinal herbs.

And don't worry, I promise you this process is neither difficult nor painful on your part.

Now that you've harvested the herbs, you'll want them to last as long as possible. The best way to do this is through a drying process. In days past, it was custom to simply hang the herbs in a warm, dry, shady location, wait until they crumbled easily and then place them in various containers.

Custom also dictated that the roots were washed, split and then spread into a single layer on a clean tray. And this method is still practiced diligently by a few herbalists. It isn't unusual to walk into an herb shop and actually buy a "bunch" of herbs.

But, that's not to say it's the best approach. In fact, there are two distinct disadvantages to using this method. First, it takes up a lot of space, sometimes more space than you can devote.

The other disadvantage is the time factor. It takes at a minimum a few days, and in some instances weeks for the leaves, stems and flowers to dry on their own. And we haven't even begun to talk about the roots, which in some instances may take up to a month or more to completely dry properly.

Time is of the Essence

When drying herbs for medicinal or healing purposes, time is literally of the essence. The faster the herbs are dried, the more potent the volatile aromatic oils in the herbs will be. And that's precisely why most of the commercial herb producers use special equipment for drying herbs.

In order to speed the process somewhat, many herb gardeners simply place their herbs on a baking sheet or on a section of clean window screen, then place this is an oven set at 95 degrees.

This method is not only convenient, but inexpensive as well. Of course, this has a few disadvantages. One of the biggest being that in the heat of summer not many people really want to use the oven to cook, let alone for drying herbs.

Moreover, if your oven is one of those that don't heat evenly, it can cause you some problems. Some of the herbs may actually dry out too much, while other sections are too moist.

So what can you do? Some herbalists buy a small produce dryer. This is a table top appliance with built-in removable trays. It uses a hot air fan to dry the herbs. As you might have already guessed by its name, it also dries produce.

Drying is Just the Beginning

Drying is just the first step in the preservation process. Once the herbs have dried, many herbalists then reduce them to a powder. This is the most convenient form for use.

Traditionally, herbalists have made their powders using the old-fashioned mortar and pestle. And it's a method that many still use today, especially if you don't have many herbs to grind.

If that seems a bit old fashioned to you, try grinding your herbs in a coffee grinder. You may want to purchase one separately for this purpose. You might not want the flavors of either mixing with the other.

For those gardeners who have large amounts of herbs, a large grinder is advisable.

Storing Your Herbs

Take a quick look at the bottled commercially bought herbs and spices you already have in your kitchen cabinet for a moment. Carefully examine the bottle they're in. Is it a clear glass or plastic bottle?

Chances are it is clear. That way you can actually see the type of spice you're purchasing. Clear bottles may even cost less than dark amber ones.

But you're about to learn a powerful lesson in preserving herbs: clear glass is the worst thing you can keep your dried herbs in. And here's why: light, the giver of life for these plants for so long, is also the destroyer of potency and flavor once the herbs are dry. It's ironic, but true.

Instead, store your dried herbs in opaque containers, glass or ceramic are best. Fill the container to the top. This limits the amount of oxygen in them. As you use your herbs, you can prevent oxygen from seeping inside by adding cotton to the jar.

Carefully stored aromatic herbs, like sage, rosemary and thyme can actually remain potent for a year and more. Expect herbs that don't carry much of a fragrance, like alfalfa to last even longer.

Moisture Kills

Moisture is another enemy of your dried herbs. If they should happen to get wet once they've been dried, quickly dry them again. This prevents the growth of mold.

You'll also want to be vigilant to the problem of insects. Drying takes care of many of the pests, but always keep an eye open for insects. To help avoid this problem, make sure the containers are tightly closed when you're not actively using your herbs.

Freezing Fresh Herbs

So far, we've discussed drying herbs to use later, especially if these are for healing purposes. But if you're storing culinary herbs, there's no reason why you just can't freeze these. This is simple and makes cooking with them during the winter easy.

Here's how to do this:

- Cut the stems or the leaves of the herbs
- Rinse them
- Pat them dry
- Freeze them in resealable bags

The bags should be small, then all you have to do is take one bag out and have just enough for your meal.

You can also freeze chopped fresh herbs in ice cube trays with water. After the water and herbs have frozen, transfer them to freezer bags. This is actually a great way to use them for soup.

Now that autumn is approaching, you've harvested and preserved your herbs, what's left to do?

Why don't you just sit down with the cup of herbal tea and plan next season's garden.

Conclusion

As I'm sure you've discovered by now, it really wasn't as difficult as you envisioned at first, was it? When approached properly, herb gardening is one of the joys of nature. It's relaxing to do and provides hours of potential peace and serenity in the growing season.

From basil to thyme, each herb has its own distinct characteristic, growing quirk and specialty on your kitchen table and for healing your body. Each herb, you've discovered, has in effect its own personality.

I certainly hope you've enjoyed learning about herbs as much as I've enjoyed writing about them. Hopefully, you'll continue on with your new hobby and discover even more about herbs next growing season.

There's always something to learn. After more years than I care to admit growing these fantastic plants, I'm still learning something new everyday about the proper way to water, harvest, store them or any number of things.

Don't become discouraged if some of your plants fizzled out this year. Certainly don't believe that your thumb isn't green enough to be an herb gardener. It happens to the best of us. It still happens to me to this day.

A certain percentage of herbs just don't seem to make it sometimes. Sometimes you know why. For instance, you've had an extremely rainy summer or didn't provide for enough drainage, for example. Other times these things just happen and leave even the best of gardeners scratching their heads in wonder.

Well, this is where I leave you. But, thankfully you're now surrounded by your herbs. Take care -- and take care of your garden. Happy gardening!

Appendix I

What Your Herbs need

Growing Requirements, Propagation and Uses of Herbs

Annual Herbs

Plant	Height	Spacing	Light Requirement	Propagation	Uses
Anise *Pimpinella anisum*	24"	10"	Sun	seed.	Leaves in soups, sauces, and salads; oil for flavoring; seeds for seasoning cakes, breads, and cookies.
Basil, sweet *Ocimum basilicum*	20 to 24"	6 to 12"	Sun	seed; grow transplants for early-season harvest.	Leaves in soups, stews, pasta sauce, poultry and meat dishes; flavors vinegar; teas.

Borage *Borago officinalis*	1 to 3'	12"	Sun	seed; self-sowing.	Edible flower; leaves in salads, teas, and sandwiches; attracts bees.
Calendula (Pot Marigold) *Calendula officinalis*	12"	12 to 18"	Sun, partial shade	seed.	Flower petals give color to soups, custards, and rice; cookies; vinegars; crafts.
Caraway *Carum carvi*	12 to 24"	10"	Sun	seed; biennial seed bearer, some cultivars are annual seed bearers.	Leaves in salads, teas, stews, and soups; seeds for flavoring cookies, breads, salads, and cheeses; roots can be cooked.
Chamomile, sweet false *Matricaria recutita*	1 to 2 ½'	4 to 6"	Sun	seed.	Tea, potpourris, garnish, crafts.
Chervil *Anthriscus cerefolium*	1 ½ to 2'	15"	Partial shade	Sow seeds in early spring; needs light to germinate; does not transplant well, not heat tolerant.	Leaves in salads, soups, and sauces; teas; butters.

Coriander (cilantro) *Coriandrum sativum*	24" to 36"	12 to 18"	Sun, partial shade	seed; goes to seed quickly, so plant frequently.	Entire plant is edible; leaves in stews and sauces; stems flavor soups and beans; seeds in sauces and meat dishes, potpourris, and sachets.
Dill *Anethum graveolens*	3 to 5'	3 to 12"	Sun, partial shade	Sow seed early spring.	Teas; seasoning for butter, cakes, bread, vinegars, soups, fish, pickles, salads, etc.; flowers in crafts.
Nasturtium *Tropaeolum* **spp.**	15"	6"	Sun	seed; does not transplant well.	Leaves, stems, and flowers have a peppery taste; use in salads.
Parsley *Petroselinum crispum*	6 to 18"	6"	Sun	Sow seed early spring; slow to germinate; soak in warm water; is a biennial grown as an annual.	Garnish; flavoring for salads, stews, soups, sauces, and salad dressings.

Perilla *Perilla frutescens*	36"	3 to 6"	Sun	seed.	Decorative plant; flavoring oriental dishes.
Summer savory *Satureja hortensis*	12 to 18"	10 to 12"	Sun	Sow seed in early spring, cuttings.	Mild peppery taste; used with meat, cabbage, rice, and bean dishes, stuffings, teas, butters, vinegars.

Biennial and Perennial Herbs

Common name/ *Scientific name*	Height	Spacing	Light Requirement	Propagation	Uses
Angelica *Angelica archangelica*	2 to 3'	3'	Partial shade	seed.	Stems raw or in salads; leaves in soups and stews; teas; crafts; closely resembles poisonous water hemlock.
Anise hyssop *Agastache foeniculum*	3 to 5'	12 to 24"	Sun, light shade	seed or division.	Attracts bees; edible flowers; leaves for flavoring or teas; crafts; seeds used in cookies, cakes, and muffins.
Artemisia *Artemisia* spp.	2 to 3'	24"	Sun, partial shade	Division.	Wreaths and other crafts; aromatic foliage.
Bee balm *Monarda didyma*	2 to 3'	12 to 15"	Sun, partial shade	seed or division; invasive rhizomes.	Attracts bees, butterflies, and hummingbirds; teas; flavors jellies, soups, stews, and fruit salads; edible flowers; dried flowers in crafts.

Burnet, salad *Poterium sanguisorba*	12"	18 to 24"	Sun, well-drained soil	seed or division.	Cucumber-flavored leaves used in salads, vinegar, butter, cottage cheese, and cream cheese; garnish.
Clary sage *Salvia sclarea*	5'	24"	Sun	seed; biennial.	Leaves in omelets, fritters, and stews; flavoring of beers and wines; oil.
Chamomile *Chamaemelum nobile*	2 to 8"	18"	Sun, partial shade; well-drained soil	seed, division, or stem cuttings.	Dried flowers for tea; potpourris; herb pillows.
Catnip *Neptea cataria*	3 to 4'	12 to 18"	Sun or shade	seed or division.	Teas; fragrance for cats.
Chives *Allium schoenoprasum*	12"	12"	Sun, partial shade	seed or division.	Edible flowers; leaves for flavoring, eggs, soups, salads, butter, cheese, dips, spreads, etc.
Comfrey *Symphythum officinale*	3 to 5'	3'	Sun	seed, cuttings, root division.	Safety of ingestion is highly questionable. Large, rambling plant; dyes, cosmetics.
Costmary *Chrysanthemum balsamita*	2 to 4'	12"	Sun, light shade	Division.	Garnish; fragrance.

Echinacea *Echinacea angustifolia*	1 to 2'	18"	Sun	seed or crown division.	Ornamental plant; used medicinally.
Fennel *Foeniculum vulgare*	4 to 5'	4 to 12"	Sun	seed, difficult to transplant.	Entire plant edible; seeds in sausage and baked goods; leaves used with fish, vegetables, cheese spreads, and soups.
Feverfew *Tanacetum parthenium*	2 to 3'	12"	Sun, partial shade	seed or division.	Tea, crafts, dyes.
Geranium, scented *Pelargonium* spp.	12 to 24"	12 to 24"	Sun	stem cuttings.	Teas, potpourris, sachets, jellies, vinegars, desserts.
Germander *Teucrium chamaedrys*	10 to 12"	8 to 10"	Sun, partial shade	Slow to germinate from seed. Stem cuttings, layering, division.	Attracts bees, decorative plant.
Horehound *Marrubium vulgare*	24"	15"	Full sun	seed, cuttings, or division.	Attracts bees; tea; flavoring in candy, crafts.
Hyssop *Hyssopus officinalis*	24"	15"	Sun	seed, stem cuttings, or division.	Attracts bees and butterflies; mostly decorative usage, potpourris.

Lavender *Lavandula angustifolia*	24 to 36"	18"	Sun	seed or stem cuttingsv	Potpourris; herb pillows; crafts, vinegars and jellies.
Lemon balm *Melissa officinalis*	3'	2'	Sun, light shade	seed, stem cuttings, or division.	Teas; flavors soups, stew, fish, poultry, vegetables, and meat dishes; garnish; potpourris.
Lemon verbena *Aloysia triphylla*	2 to 5'	12 to 24"	Sun	stem cuttings.	Potpourris; herb pillows; lemon flavoring for drinks, salads, and jellies; teas.
Lovage *Levisticum officinale*	3 to 5'	2'	Sun, partial shade	Sow seeds late summer; division.	Seeds in breads, butters, and cakes; teas; leaves in soup, stew, cheese, cookies, and chicken dishes; root edible.
Marjoram *Majorana hortensis*	1 to 2'	12"	Sun	stem cuttings, division, or seed.	Flavoring for meats, salads, omelets, vinegars; jellies; teas; flower head for crafts.

Oregano *Origanum vulgare* and *O. vulgare* subsp. *hirtum*	24"	8 to 12"	Sun	Grow from cuttings or division.	Flavoring for tomato dishes, meat, poultry and pork stuffings; vegetables and sauces, etc.
Peppermint *Mentha x piperita*	36"	18"	Sun, light shade	Cuttings and division recommended; invasive rhizomes.	Teas, fragrance.
Rosemary *Rosemarinus officinalis*	3 to 6'	12"	Sun	Seeds slow to germinate; use stem cuttings, layering, or division.	Teas; flavoring for vinegar, jam, bread, butters, stuffing, vegetables, stew, and meat dishes.
Rue *Ruta graveolens*	3'	12 to 18"	Sun	seed, stem cuttings, or division.	Decorative plant.
Sage *Salvia officinalis*	18 to 30'	12"	Sun	Grows slowly from seed; stem cuttings, division, layering.	Seasoning for meat, vegetable and egg dishes; stuffings.
Sage, pineapple *Salvia elegans*	2 to 3'	24"	Sun	Stem cuttings.	Attracts hummingbirds and butterflies; teas; potpourri; cream cheese; jams, jellies.

Santolina *Santolina chamaecyparissus*	24"	2 to 3'	Sun, needs good drainage	Slow to germinate from seeds. Stem cuttings, layering, or division.	Dried arrangements and potpourris; accent plant.
Sorrel *Rumex* spp.	3 to 4'	12"	Sun	seed.	Flavoring of soups, butters, omelets; some species of sorrel are toxic.
Southernwood *Artemisia abrotanum*	4'	18"	Sun, well drained soil	Stem cuttings, division.	Teas; sachets; potpourris.
Spearmint *Mentha spicata*	18"	18"	Sun, partial shade	Cuttings or division recommended; invasive rhizomes.	Teas; flavors sauces, jellies, and vinegars; leaves in fruit salad, peas, etc.
Sweet marjoram *Origanum majorana*	8"	12"	Sun	seed, division, or cuttings.	Flavors tomato sauces, eggs, etc. Leaves in salads, sauces, pizza, and meats.
Sweet rocket *Hesperis matronalis*	3 to 4'	24"	Sun	seed.	Salads.
Sweet woodruff *Galium odoratum*	8"	12"	Partial shade	Division.	Tea; sachets, dyes.
Tansy *Tanacetum vulgare*	3 to 4'	2 to 3'	Sun	seed or division.	Toxic oil in leaves; decorative plant; crafts.

Tarragon *Artemisia dracunculus*	24"	12"	Sun	Division or root cuttings, stem cuttings are slow to root.	Sauces, salads, soups, omelets, meat, vegetable, and fish dishes.
Thyme, common *Thymus vulgaris*	4 to 12"	6 to 12"	Sun	Cuttings, seeds, or division.	Teas; attracts bees; sachets; potpourris; flavoring for poultry, fish, stews, soups, tomatoes, cheese, eggs, and rice.
Valerian *Valeriana officinalis*	2 to 5'	12 to 24"	Sun	Division is recommended over seeding.	Roots for flavoring; ornamental plant.
Yarrow *Achillea millefolium*	8" to 5'	12"	Sun	Seeds or division.	Crafts.
Winter savory *Satureja montana*	24"	18"	Sun	Grow in light, sandy soil from cuttings or seed; cut out dead wood.	Leaves used to flavor meat, fish, salads, soup, stew, and sausage.
Wormwood *Artemisia absinthium*	36"	12 to 36"	Sun	Seed germinate slowly; use stem cuttings or division.	Bitter flavor; toxic if consumed in large quantity; ornamental plant, dried arrangements; insect repellent.

Appendix II

Preparing Herbal Remedies

As you prepare your home-grown herbs to be used as remedies, remember that you are continuing a tradition that's as old as mankind himself. It's exciting (and quite humbling) to be part of a heritage that actually goes back to the Stone Age.

Herbs can be used to heal in a variety of ways. Here's how you heal yourself, your family and your friends by using a tincture-based herb.

A tincture is a preserved form of the herb, using some form of alcohol as the preservative. But more than that, the alcohol is used to extract the active properties of the herb as well as concentrate them to ensure their effectiveness.

A tincture also has the advantage of being very easy for your body to use. Tinctures are indeed both concentrated and cost-effective.

There is one downside to them, however. When you drink a tincture, you receive the full flavor of the herb. And for some people this taste will be just too much. Some people may find this just downright unpleasant. Cayenne for example, will come through very hot. Goldenseal, when used in a tincture has an extremely bitter taste.

Of course, the presence of the alcohol in this form of herbal preparation may bother right from the start. Quite frankly, I don't blame you one bit if it does.

This is of special concern many times for parents. They would love to give their children a serving of the tincture herb to make them feel better, but they're fearful of the alcohol content of it. Some herbalists say that you can just lessen the concentration of the alcohol in the tincture by mixing the serving with one-quarter cup of very hot water.

Wait about five minutes, and then most of that alcohol taste will have evaporated. And the tincture should be cool enough to drink.

Making your own tincture:

- Dried or fresh herbs
- 80 to 100 proof vodka or rum (Never use rubbing alcohol, also known as Isopropyl Alcohol or wood alcohol)
- Wide-mouth glass jar with lid (a canning jar is perfect)
- Unbleached cheesecloth or muslin
- Labels
- Markers
- Small amber glass bottles

Tincture Recipe

The exact amount of the individual herb you use is up to you, depending on the amount of tincture you have on hand. A good rule of thumb is to use one part herb to every five parts of alcohol. It really doesn't matter how large that "part" is.

Place your finely chopped herbs into the canning jar. Pour the alcohol in the ratio advised into the jar. Make sure the alcohol base completely covers your herb.

Now close the lid tightly. Allow the herbs to soak for up to six wecks. During this time, make sure you shake the jar every few days. The alcohol siphons and extracts the active ingredients from the herbs during this period.

At the end of six weeks, use a large sieve, strainer or other type of press to strain the mixture. Immediately take the wet herbs, wrapping them in muslin, cheesecloth or another type of fine cloth. Tightly but gently squeeze the herbs to get as much of the alcohol-based mixture off the herbs as possible.

The herbs that are the most saturated will naturally also be those that are strongest when it comes to carrying the active medicinal ingredients of healing power.

Your next step is to take the herbs from your large container and place them in smaller glass bottles. Preferably, the bottles should be amber colored.

That's it. You've made your first tincture from your own herbs grown in your own garden.

By the by the way, the tincture you made today will be effective for up to five years.

Herbal Plasters

Okay, so the first time I heard this phrase I thought it meant a cast of some sort. But nothing can be farther from the truth. It actually has little to do with plaster in any sense that you may be thinking about.

But, a plaster is a thick, moist herbal paste that's warmed and placed between two layers of cheesecloth or muslin. Some herbalists us a cloth pouch. This is then placed directly on the skin where the irritation is. The herb itself, because it is wrapped in the cloth never actually touches the skin. For this reason you need to be very careful in using one of these.

Most frequently used in the treatment of respiratory congestion, a plaster can also be used for such conditions as skin infections, irritable bowel syndrome and even high blood pressure.

Plasters work well because they release their oils which contain the healing ingredients.

When making a plaster, your first step is to grind your herb (preferably a dried herb) *immediately prior* to actually preparing the remedy itself. The grinding of the herb releases the pockets of enzymes which in turn activates the essential oils of the plant.

Once you've ground your home-grown herbs, then you mix about ¼ cup (roughly 2 ounces) of the herb in just enough lukewarm water (never hot for this preparation) to make a thick paste-like concoction. *Do not get this mixture in your eyes or under your fingernails.*

Take this paste-like mixture and place it between several layers of clean cloth, such as cheesecloth or muslin. Place the plaster over the affected area of the body.

After about five minutes, you'll notice a burning sensation. Don't be alarmed; this is part of the healing process. It's merely a signal that the herbal oils are penetrating the deeper layers of your skin.

Once this burning sensation begins though, you should remove the herbal plaster immediately. You have a window of about five to 15 minutes when it can safely stay on your body. But 15 minutes is really the very maximum.

A word of Caution: if you have a circulatory problem, herbalist and nutritionist, Phyllis Balch advises in her book *Prescriptions for herbal Healing* not to use a plaster for any reason.

Poultices

An herbal poultice is nothing more than a thick, moist, warm herbal paste applied directly to the skin.

Its purpose is to relieve pain, inflammation as well as swelling or muscle spasms. You make poultices with your homegrown herbs, either while they are still fresh or after you've dried them.

To create a healing poultice from dried herbs, place a steamer, heat-proof colander, a strainer or even a sieve over a pot of rapidly boiling water. Place up to 2 ounces (¼ cup) of your herb in the container. Cover the pot and reduce the heat under the water so it just simmers.

Allow the steam to penetrate through the herbs until they are wilted. This should occur within five minutes. Then spread the softened, warmed herbs on cheesecloth, folding one layer of the cloth over the herb itself.

Apply this directly to affected area of your body. If you'd like, you can cover the poultice with a towel or even a woolen cloth. This will help it to retain the heat longer.

The poultice can remain in place for at least twenty minutes. In fact, you may even leave it on overnight but it must be covered.

If you prefer to make your pulped poultice from fresh herbs, place the herbs between two layers of cheesecloth that is twice the size of the area affected. Take a rolling pin or other equally heavy round object and finely crush the herbs. You'll know that the herbs are sufficiently crushed when the cloth feels damp from the moisture of the herbs themselves.

If you have a food processer, you may want to place the herbs in that. Then mix a small amount of hot water with them.

Now place a towel or woolen cloth over this to retain the "juices" and to help to hold the herbs in place. A poultice like this may also remain on the affected area overnight, if necessary.

The key to a poultice's effectiveness is that you use these particular set of herbs only once. Don't try to store a used poultice and use it again. Toss it and start all over again the following day or even several hours later.

References

Web Sites

http://www.Herbpalace.com

http://www.TheEpicentre.com

http://www.Alchemy-Works.com

http://www.Flower-Gardening-Made-Easy.com

http://www.Nutrasanus.com

http://www.AltNature.com

http://www.Essential-Herb-Garden.com

http://www.PlantCare.com

http://www.PlanetNatural.com

http://www.HerbGardeningTips.com/

Books

Hanson, Beth, **Designing an herb garden**, Brooklyn Botanic Gardens, New York City, NY, 2004.

Caduto, Michael J., ***Everyday Herbs in Spiritual Life,*** Skylight Paths Publishing, Woodstock, VT

Castleman, Michael, ***The New Healing Herbs,*** 2001

Index

A

Anemia, *31*
Anise, *28*
Antioxidants, *31*
Aphids, *33, 64, 66*
Apple trees, *67*
Aromatic herbs, *16 23, 46, 87*
Arthritis, *31, 41*
Asian dishes, *25*
Asparagus, *67*
Aspirin, *20*

B

Basil, *11, 14, 16, 24, 43-44, 50, 52-53, 55, 60, 66, 89*
Beans, *65, 67, 93*
Beetles, *64*
Bible, *15*
Bird baths, *57*
Broccoli, *67*
Burdock, *33*

C

Cabbage, *66-68, 94*
Calendula, *32*
Carrots, *67-68*
Casseroles, *27*
Caterpillars, *64*
Catnip, *52, 60*
Chamomile, *35, 60*
Cheese dishes, *24, 28-29*
Chinese, *15, 18, 22*
Chives, *14, 17, 24, 67*
Cold drinks, *26*
Collard, *67*
Companion plants, *65-66*
Container gardens, *13*
Containers, *10, 21, 53, 61, 63, 70, 74, 76, 84, 87*
Corn, *65, 67*

Cream cheese, *24, 96, 99*
Cucumber, *68*
Culinary herbs, *14*

D

Design a Garden, *11, 43*
Dill, *25, 67*
Dittany of Crete, *17*
Drying herbs, *85, 87*

E

Echinacea, *20, 21, 36- 38, 46*
Egyptians, *14, 16*
England, *35*
Ephedra. See Ma Huang

F

Fennel, *26-67*
Fertilization, *62, 75*
Feverfew, *40-41, 97*
Flavonoids, *31*
Flies, *66*
Flower garden, *10, 52, 65*
Fluorescent Light, *71- 73*
Foot candles, *72-73*
Fungicide, *75*

G

Garden plots, *49*
Gardening magazines, *47*
Garlic, *65, 67*
Ginger, *83*
Ginseng, *83-84*
Greenhouse, *24*

H

Hardening off, *61-62*
Harvesting, *31*, *35*, *79*, *82-83*
Healing Herbs, *30*, *110*
Healthy blood pressure, *38*
Hedges, *56*
Herbal medicine. *See* Medicinal Herbs
High-intensity discharge light, *71*
Humidity, *74*

I

Indian dishes, *25*
Indoor, *11*, *70*, *71*, *74*
Inflammation, *31*, *107*
Insecticidal soap, *33*, *64*
Insomnia, *38*

J

Japanese, *22*

K

Knot garden, *51*
Kyphi, *16*

L

Lamb, *26*, *28-29*
Lavender, *37*, *98*
Lemon balm, *39*
Lettuce, *67*
Lovage, *16*
Lupus, *31*

M

Ma huang., *18*
Mandrake, *83*
Marigold, *32*
Marjoram, **16**, *60*, *100*
Marshmallow root, *18*
Medicinal herbs, *17*, *21*, *31*, *49*, *50*, *84*

Medieval, *48*, *50-51*
Migraine headache, *40*
Mint, *17*, *26*, *67*
Mites, *64*, *67*
Mortar and pestle, *86*
Mosquitoes, *66*
Mulch, *63-64*, *81*
Muscle relaxant, *38*
Muscle spasms, *107*

N

Neighboring plants, *27*
Nettles, *31*
Nursery, *23*, *28-29*, *38*, *63*, *64*, *71*, *75-76*

O

Omelets, *25*, *27*, *96*, *98*, *100-101*
Oregano, *14*, *17*, *60*, *67*, *81*
Ornamental herbs, *17*
Outdoor garden, *11*, *60*, *62*

P

Parsley, *15*, *27*, *43*, *52*, *55*, *67*
Plastic bucket, *27*
Poultice, *12*, *107-108*
Powdery mildew disease, *67*, *77*
Preserving, *79*, *82*, *84*, *86*
Propagating herbs, **82**
Pruning, *80*
Purple Coneflower. *See* Echinacea

R

Rainfall, *64*
Remedies, *12*, *35*, *37*, *103*
Renaissance, *48*, *50*
Respiratory congestion, *105*
Rheumatism, *41*
Root rot, *74*, *80-81*
Rosemary, *16*, *29*, *53*, *55*, *68*, *81*, *87*
Roses, *52*, *65*

S

Sage, *27-28, 50, 53, 67-68, 87, 96, 99*
Salads, *24-28, 34, 91-93, 95-96, 98, 100-101*
Sandwich filling, *24-25*
Sauces, *24, 91-93, 99-100*
Seeds, *14, 24-29, 32, 34-35, 37-39, 41, 44, 47, 60, 72, 76, 83-84, 91-93, 95, 97-98, 100-101*
Sorrel, *60, 100*
Soups, *24-26, 28-29, 34, 91-93, 95-98, 100-101*
Squash, *65-66*
St. John's wort, *40*
Stomach cramps, *41*
Strawberries, *66*

T

Tarragon, *28*
Tea garden, *22, 55-57*
Teapots, *56*
Thyme, *17, 29, 53, 55, 60, 68, 87, 89*
Tincture, *12, 103-105*
Tomatoes, *66-67, 101*
Trellises, *56*

V

Valerian, *41-42, 101*
Verilux tubes, *72*
Vinegar, *28, 91, 96, 99*

Printed in Poland
by Amazon Fulfillment
Poland Sp. z o.o., Wrocław